THE
SPIRITUAL TEACHINGS
OF
RALPH WALDO EMERSON

THE
SPIRITUAL TEACHINGS
OF
RALPH WALDO EMERSON

Richard Geldard

With a Foreword by

Robert Richardson

LINDISFARNE BOOKS

\10\|0")

Published by Lindisfarne Books
PO Box 799, Great Barrington, MA 01230
www.lindisfarne.org

Library of Congress Cataloging-in-Publication Data

Geldard, Richard G., 1935–
    The spiritual teachings of Ralph Waldo Emerson / Richard
Geldard; with a foreword by Robert Richardson.
X, 196 p. cm.
    Rev. ed. of Esoteric Emerson. c 1993.
    Includes bibliographical references and index.
    ISBN 0-9701097-3-3
    1. Emerson, Ralph Waldo, 1803–1882 — Religion. 2. Spiritual life in
literature. 3. Religion in literature. I. Geldard, Richard G. 1935– Esoteric
Emerson. II. Title.

PS1642.R4 G44 2001
814'.3 — dc21   00-054458

10 9 8 7 6 5 4 3 2

Printed in the United States of America

TABLE OF CONTENTS

FOREWORD

No one who has felt the life-changing pull of Emerson's enormous planetary mind has ever doubted his power or his greatness, though we are often puzzled to know whether he is primarily a poet, an essayist or a philosopher. Richard Geldard is not puzzled at all by this; he has written a book which plainly shows the essential Emerson to be a teacher, the Socrates of Concord, a man with a message that we need to hear today. Previous generations "beheld God and nature face to face," Emerson says, and he adds, provocatively, that we moderns seem able only to see those things through the eyes of the earlier generations. "Why," he asks—and the question is intended to shatter our complacency—"Why should not we also enjoy an original relation to the universe? Why should not we have a poetry and philosophy of insight and not of tradition, and a religion by revelation to us, and not the history of theirs?"

Emerson's life was devoted to showing how one may still attain an original, that is to say, an authentic, relation to the universe, and Geldard's book aims to focus and distill the famously dispersed Emerson and put his central teachings into the modern reader's hand. Geldard understands the main thing, which is that Emerson is as alive, as pertinent, as urgent now as he was in his lifetime. We have only to reach out for the gifts which Emerson, like a new god on a new day, offers us.

Where to begin? "Where do we find ourselves?" is Emerson's way of starting. "We awake," he says,"and find ourselves on a stair; there are stairs below us, which we seem to have ascended; there are stairs above us, many a one, which go upward and out of sight" It is a scene from Piranesi's Imaginary Prisons, where stairs spiral up and reel down, and end in blank walls, in mid-air, or in darkness. Emerson's intended audience is not a crowd or a group, but always the solitary reader, imprisoned, it may be, by the past, or by family, or habit, or fear of the future. Where do we find ourselves? Not in the nineteenth century, not in Concord (or not only there), not among men only, nor among white people only. We find ourselves, says Emerson, one by one in the here and now. "We must set up the strong present tense against all the rumors of wrath, past or to come."

Emerson's central message, as William James understood it and as Van Wyck Brooks summed it up, is the same message that "has marked all the periods of revival, the early Christian Age and Luther's age, Rousseau's, Kant's and Goethe's, namely, that the innermost nature of things is congenial to the powers that men possess." Six months after the death of his first child, Waldo, aged five, Emerson rose in his grief to write to a Quaker acquaintance in Baltimore, Solomon Corner, that he, Emerson, had got no further than his old conviction that the powers of the soul are commensurate with its needs, all experience to the contrary notwithstanding."

If true, why is this not more quickly apparent to us? Because, as Emerson fully recognized, something has gone wrong. It is literally true, as Emerson says and as Geldard emphasizes, that each of us "is made of the same atoms as the world is." "We are star-stuff," as Carl Sagan liked to say. "Except for hydrogen," he wrote, "all the atoms that make each of us up—the iron in our blood, the calcium in our bones, the carbon in our brains—were manufactured in red giant stars thousands of light years away in space and billions of years ago in time." Each new person is a fresh assortment of atoms and, as Emerson says, "the power which resides in him is new in nature." But we have lost our vital connections to our heritage, like the orphan in a Victorian novel, and our task is now for each of us to regain his or her proper place in the world. "The reason why the world lacks unity, and lies broken and in heaps," says Emerson, "is because man is disunited with himself."

The solution is self-reliance. "To believe your own thought, to believe that what is true for you in your private heart is true for all men,–that is genius." Fair enough, we say, but how exactly does one go about gaining this belief? We expect Emerson to lead us through, say, a twelve-step program, forgetting that what Emerson has to give us is the source, the secret, the reason why twelve-step programs work in the first place. We want a solid, should I say material, program from Emerson, but the basic fact is that "the foundations of man are not in matter, but in spirit," as Emerson flatly puts it in Nature. The vital principle, the source of power for the human being, is the soul.

Now this is precisely the strength of Richarld Geldard's book, that he fully and sympathetically understands this spiritual dimension in Emerson, just as he honors and praises the work of other and earlier teachers of the same doctrine, such as Plotinus and Thomas Taylor. The Emersonian work we must do to be saved is spiritual work. And for that spiritual work, Geldard's is the most practical and useful handbook we have apart from Emerson's own writings. Geldard leads the reader to a solid grasp of such concepts as "lowly listening," "opening the heart," to how "the best we can say of God is the mind as it is known to us," and finally to an understanding that courage, meaning "equality to the problem before us," is possible for us too. Geldard restores Emerson to the position he held among his contemporaries, that of a "seer of a revolution in human self-recovery."

Emerson believes, and make bring us to believe, that we have it in us to lead better lives, that we too can "affect the quality of the day," as his friend Henry Thoreau put it. And while all

Emerson's teaching is based on the importance and power of the spirit, the means and the results are often surprisingly tangible. Even such a statement as "hitch your wagon to a star," which sounds impractical if beautiful, turns out to have an unexpected grounding in the real world. Emerson was thinking, when he wrote that phrase, about the tide-mills that used to exist in Boston and along the East Coast. A dam, with a mill and a water wheel, would be built across the mouth of a long narrow bay. The incoming tide would turn the wheel one way, the outgoing tide would turn it the other way; both ways ground grain and sawed wood, and it was all done by hitching the mill to the tides which are hitched to the moon. So Emerson means his spiritual advice literally when he says—and we must hear where the emphasis falls —"hitch your wagon to a star." Richard Geldard will show you how to tie the hitch.

— Robert Richardson

INTRODUCTION

It has been one hundred and fifty
years since the powerful, startling messages from the pen of
Ralph Waldo Emerson began to flow out of Concord,
Massachusetts, to a small circle of devoted readers in America
and England. After his death in 1882, American culture
subsumed much of that power into the broader, pragmatic
vision of individualism and expansionism, and the man who was
once understood as the seer of a revolution in human self-
recovery was more weakly read as America's beloved idealist.

In the first half of the nineteenth century, however, Emerson
was indeed a radical reformer, not in terms of social values and
literary taste, but for his perception of human nature. The
clearest articulation of the difference appeared in "Man the
Reformer:"

> What is a man born for but to be a Reformer, a Re-maker
> of what man has made; a renouncer of lies; a restorer of
> truth and good, imitating that great Nature which embo-
> soms us all, and which sleeps no moment on an old past,
> but every hour repairs herself, yielding us every morning a
> new day, and with every pulsation a new life? Let him re-
> nounce everything which is not true to him, and put all his

1

practices back on their first thoughts, and do nothing for which he has not the whole world for his reason. If there are inconveniences, and what is called ruin in the way, because we have so enervated and maimed ourselves, yet it would be like dying of perfumes to sink in the effort to reattach the deeds of every day to the holy and mysterious recesses of life.

("Man the Reformer")

The sources of reform for Emerson were these "holy and mysterious recesses of life," at the depth of which lay the foundations of culture and the limits of human consciousness. This passage, like so many from his work, striking again and again at the surfaces of our perceptions, marks Emerson as a purveyor of radically new and yet ancient esoteric knowledge which has threaded its way from the recesses of pre-history into the sacred texts of Egypt, to the Hindu Vedas and Upanishads, through Greek Orphic texts to Pythagoras and Plato and the Neoplatonists and thence to our own age through a thin line of similar reformers. It is not precisely what has been called by some the Perennial Philosophy, nor is it simply Neoplatonism dressed up as German Transcendentalism, nor is it the muted Idealism of Kant. Rather, the radical thought which took root in Emerson had its basis in a carefully wrought definition of mind in nature and mind as a universal faculty, whose characteristics and power were to be the foundation of an evolved human culture, and for Emerson a life-long teaching.

As a teacher, Emerson left for his pupils a complete and complex record of his life and thought. He left us hundreds of private journals, the raw material of his lectures, essays and poems, six volumes of letters, and the *Works of Emerson,* a compendium of essays and speeches collected under his supervision and editorial control. The original was published in 1903. More recently, the Harvard University Press has been publishing an updated, thoroughly annotated *Collected Works,* which when complete will be a great aid to scholars. The Library of America volume entitled *Emerson* is the most complete collection in print in one volume of the essays and lectures. In addition, there have been gathered over the years his early lectures and sermons, which give us an indication of the development of his thought.[1]

Emerson's intellectual and personal life are well documented and collected. Numerous biographies are available. The Houghton Library at Harvard University has in its holdings most of Emerson's personal library and a good record of his reading habits, particularly in his formative years. We know, for example, how he marked and noted passages in his edition of Plato's works. We know what books he borrowed from area libraries as a young man and how he used these materials to find his intellectual way in the world.

Emerson's personal biography reveals a man who knew early hardship, both in terms of family tragedy and personal illness. His father died when Waldo was nearly eight, leaving a widow, five sons, and a daughter to survive on the generosity of church fathers and a boarding house income. The daughter, Mary Caroline, died in 1814, and one of the boys, Robert Bulkeley Emerson, was mentally incompetent and would need institutional care for most of his life. The struggling family lived in a rambling house on Hancock Street in a poor section of Boston, where young Waldo often went to school without a coat in winter. Despite serious deprivations, he received a solid classical education at the Boston Latin School and entered Harvard in 1817 on scholarship at the age of fourteen.

Fighting poor health and the uncertainties of the future, Emerson taught school after Harvard and finally followed his

---

1. Since there are so many texts of Emerson's essays available to the reading public, the author has chosen to indicate in the text only the title of the essay or poem quoted in the text. In the case of journal entries, however, the designation *JMN* is the standard reference to *The Journals and Miscellaneous Notebooks of Ralph Waldo Emerson*, Harvard University Press.

father's example by preparing for the ministry. Ordained in 1826, he reluctantly accepted the post of Junior Minister at the famous Second Church of Boston. In 1829 he married the beautiful but frail Ellen Tucker, and they shared a brief happy marriage, during which Ellen was in good health for only three brief happy months, before she died of tuberculosis in 1831. Following Ellen's death, Emerson resigned his post at Second Church, convinced of his fundamental unsuitability for the formalities of religion and set sail for Europe on December 25, 1832.

His European education included visits to Malta, Rome, Florence, Paris, and London. While in England he met the giants of his youthful reading, Coleridge, Wordsworth and Thomas Carlyle. In Carlyle he found a kindred spirit, although not the soul-mate and teacher he was seeking. During his journey he began work on his first book *Nature*, and returned to America to settle permanently in Concord. In 1833 he began his new career as a lecturer with a series entitled "The Uses of Natural History." *Nature* was published in Boston in 1836 and signals the point around which the great circle of American Transcendental thought was to be inscribed.

After settling in Concord, Emerson married Lydia Jackson and began to raise a family. His first child, Waldo Jr., died of scarlet fever at the age of five, but he and Lydia had three more children, Ellen, Edith and Edward. The Concord home became the center of intellectual life in New England, attracting Thoreau, Margaret Fuller, William Channing, Bronson Alcott, and others who became part of the Concord circle. The middle decades of the nineteenth century saw Emerson lecture throughout the country, publish extensively, and become the dominant figure in American letters.

Emerson died peacefully at his Concord home of pneumonia at 8:50 PM on April 27, 1882, at the age of seventy-nine. Perhaps the most remarkable testament of his life came from Oliver Wendell Holmes, whose memorial to Emerson (*Ralph Waldo Emerson*, 1885) captured what many observers felt to be his spiritual qualities and ethereal nature:

Emerson's earthly existence was in the estimate of his own philosophy so slight an occurrence in his career of being that his relations to the accidents of time and space seem quite secondary matters to one who has been long living in the companionship of his thought. Still, he had to be born, to take in his share of the atmosphere in which we are all immersed, to have dealings with the world of phenomena, and at length to let them all "soar and sing" as he left his earthly halfway house. It is natural and pardonable that we should like to know the details of the daily life which the men whom we admire have shared with common mortals, ourselves among the rest. But Emerson has said truly, "Great geniuses have the shortest biographies. Their cousins can tell you nothing about them. They lived in their writings, and so their home and street life was trivial and commonplace."

1

THE ACT OF REFLECTION

W here do we find ourselves?"
Emerson asks to begin his essay "Experience." Initially, this is
not an esoteric question. He is not asking us what secret
source we might search out in order to discover our true
nature—at least not at first. His more pragmatic question asks
us to locate ourselves in experience. He answers his question
with an image, suggesting that we find ourselves halfway up a
staircase, uncertain of our destination at the top (assuming
always that we are ascending) and forgetful of the steps taken
at the bottom. The question is also not merely a cultural one.
He is not speaking of America at mid-nineteenth century or
even of his own Concord circle. His question is directed to
those who are imprisoned spiritually; it is personal, individual,
and the help that emerges in the rest of the essay is given in
terms of the stages of individual consciousness, the first stage
of which is understanding the nature and function of mind.

Variations on this fundamental question are: What is our
mental state? In what sort of imaginative world do we reside?
How aware are we of our intellectual condition? Emerson was
one of a small band of thinkers and writers whose contributions
to human knowledge and understanding are measured in
moments of intuitive self-reflection. For example, the first paragraph of "Spiritual Laws" has the power to bring to stillness a

mind agitated by questions of being and at the same time to create a sense of perspective in agitated circumstances.

> When the act of reflection takes place in the mind, when we look at ourselves in the light of thought, we discover that our life is embosomed in beauty. Behind us, as we go, all things assume pleasing forms, as clouds do far off.... For it is only the finite that has wrought and suffered; the infinite lies stretched in smiling repose. ("Spiritual Laws")

The emphasis and power to create this repose lies in what Emerson calls "the act of reflection." By this he means a quality of meditative thought, characterized by an undirected waiting upon the mind to form and respond to its own laws. The relation Emerson establishes initially is between thought and being as we see in the second paragraph of "Experience," which begins with one of those thorny sentences that challenge our state of attention: "If any of us knew what we were doing, or where we are going, then when we think[,] we best know!" The implication in that conditional "if" is that we don't often know either what we are doing or where we are going; but *if*, by some chance of wakefulness, we find ourselves in the reflective state, then we have a chance of knowing something about action and direction, and about why we are on the stairs and where they might be leading us. We think; therefore we know that we are, and perhaps (somewhere on a landing) what we are doing. But there is much more to say about the sort of reflective thought that yields genuine knowledge.

When Descartes said "I think; therefore I am," he intended a similar reflection on the relation of thought to an awareness of being. He was not exclusively taking a stand on the question of existence and essence, on the chicken-and-egg question of which came first in human evolution. Descartes was asserting as firmly as he could that meaningful human existence depends upon the preeminence of conscious thought. In essence, he was saying that knowing I think gives me knowledge of my being. *Cogito ergo sum*, then, becomes more a question of metaphysics than of evolutionary doctrine. In other words, it is not a reductionist statement.

In terms of the philosophy of being, the question of where we find ourselves is a real one. Arising from it are answers to what the cosmos is, what forces brought it into existence and what, individually, happens to be our purpose in living. Emerson asks that fundamental question in a hundred different ways and opens our attention to possible answers.

What makes Emerson seminal in American letters and significant in world literature and thought is his concern throughout for the state of our perceptions. He tells us again and again that we can know through an intuition found in wakefulness (the state of reflection and the consciousness of presence), that there are laws that frame the universe and human life and that those laws can be not only known but followed. When he wrote "Experience," in late 1843 or early 1844, he had seen that the single greatest barrier to accomplishment, understanding and growth in being was sleep—not, of course, the natural rest of the body at night, but rather the ignorant sleep of the mind during the day. Not only was he speaking about the examined life (after Socrates), but also about an awareness of existence on a moment-by-moment basis, the fundamental but rare sense of presence that animates an authentic life.

There is an important connection between the authentic life we seek and the examined life we experience. Since Socrates first proposed that the unexamined life was not worth having (or living), human beings have explored the philosophical implications of the examined life. Harvard professor Robert Nozick states the task very simply in the opening sentence of *The Examined Life*. "I want to think about living and what is important in life, to clarify my thinking—and also my life." As a professional philosopher, the serious thinker like Nozick is meant to engage in an active thinking about life in order to clarify it and perhaps discover its meaning and proper direction.

But what of the so-called ordinary human being, struggling to survive, seeking a few quiet moments after a long day, filling the cluttered mind with a few strains of soothing music or a few grains of soothing alcohol? What has he or she to do with such deliberate thought? When we hear Thoreau's fierce determination in *Walden* to "live deliberately, to confront only the essential facts of life, and see if I could not learn what it had to teach," we marvel at his clarity of mind and passion to "live deep and suck out all the marrow of life," and then, perhaps we decide, in these horrific times, to leave the marrow sucking to someone else.

Thoreau's determination to live consciously may seem outlandish or impossible at first, but what philosophers, mystics, and radical individualists like Thoreau are all saying and advocating in their own deliberate lives is a certain daily, moment-driven stance within the mind, at the heart of things where, as Emerson says, "the infinite lies stretched in smiling repose."

A PLACE TO STAND

By 1823, when he was twenty years old, Waldo, as he now called himself, had graduated from Harvard and had been teaching school for two years. It was a time for taking stock, for considering his options. He had begun to keep journals some four years before, as a junior in college, and we have from that point on an excellent record of his intellectual and spiritual development. Up to 1823 his journal entries were not spectacular, except in the sense of the generally high level of his youthful perceptions and the obvious maturity of his personal observations. They were also romantic, having a tendency to imaginative myth-making and poetic longing.

After the school term that summer Emerson decided to take a solitary journey, an extended walk through Western Massachusetts and parts of Connecticut. His journal entries

include a description of a side trip near Northampton, Massachusetts, in the company of a contemporary named Allen
Strong, to a small lead mine, operated by a lone miner, who
lived with his family in a hut near the entrance to the mine.
The description of the visit to the mine displays the young
Emerson's awareness of the mythic significance of this under-
world adventure and of its place in his current psychic explorations. The entry is printed in Joel Porte's *Emerson in His
Journals* (p. 34), and describes how the two young men found
the mine, which was dug horizontally into the mountainside,
how they fired a gun at the entrance to attract the miner to
the entrance, how he arrived by means of a boat, and how
they journeyed, like young Greek heroes, to the end of the
shaft:

We welcomed the Miner to the light of the Sun and
leaving our hats without, & binding our heads we lay down
in the boat and were immediately introduced to a cave
varying in height from 4 to 6 & 8 feet, hollowed in a pretty
soft sandstone through which the water continually drops.
When we lost sight of the entrance & saw only this gloomy
passage by the light of lamps it required no effort of
imagination to believe we were leaving the world, & our
smutty ferryman was a true Charon. After sailing a few
hundred feet the vault grew higher & wider overhead &
there was a considerable trickling of water on our left; this
was the ventilator of the mine & reaches up to the surface
of the earth. We continued to advance in this manner for
900 feet & then got out of the boat & walked on planks a
little way to the end of this excavation. Here we expected
to find the lead vein & the operations of the subterranean
man, but were sadly disappointed. He had been digging
through this stone for twelve years, & has not yet
discovered any lead at all. Indications of some lead at the
surface led some Boston gentleman to set this man at work
in the expectation that after cutting his dark canal for

1000 feet, he would reach the vein, & the canal would then draw off the water which prevented them from digging from above. As yet, he has found no lead but, as he gravely observed, "has reached some excellent granite." In this part of the work he has 40 dollars for every foot he advances and it occupies him ten days to earn this. He has advanced 975 feet & spends his days, winter & summer, alone in this damp & silent tomb. He says the place is excellent for meditation, & that he sees no goblins.

Evelyn Barish, in her *Emerson, The Roots of Prophecy,* points out quite correctly that this visit came for Emerson at the time when he was searching for the foundations of his thought and that this whole period was critical to what later emerged as his essential world view:

> This "subterranean man" endlessly tunneling through an existence whose only reward was consciousness, its "excellen[ce] for meditation," is an analog resonant with broader meaning. A few weeks after returning from his journey, Emerson in his journal described man as a slave who glances upward at freedom and then returns to the hammering of his chains. Freedom and slavery were much on Waldo's mind, but consciousness, the first step toward freedom, was not readily achieved; waking up was not easy.
>
> (Barish, p. 116)

Emerson's passion for wakefulness poured out into his journal during this period and his reading shifted from history to philosophy and the Classics. In October, reflecting on the average human being's extraordinary resistance to change in the face of known facts, he wrote:

> All this passes in their minds, but they will not forsake for a day or an hour the dull unsatisfactory world to which

their customs & feelings cling & which passes before them daily in an uniform & joyless reverie. They will wait in expectation of this admonishing judgement—but they will not awake & reform. (*JMN*, II, p. 160)

This passionate realization of the presence in every moment of the potential of spiritual self-recovery was accompanied by a new sound in the journals, an authenticity of expression and connection that signaled a new confidence in Emerson's social interactions as well as a new direction in his thought. He had discovered a foundation upon which to begin to build his life.

The first indication occurs in a December 1823 journal entry. In this period he was studying the Greek philosopher Archimedes and was powerfully influenced by the well-known dictum, "Give me a place to stand and I will move the Earth." Emerson took the idea beyond its surface application as a law of engineering leverage to its more philosophic meaning (which Archimedes also must have had in mind). He assumed that Archimedes was speaking about philosophic detachment and anchoring of life in value, resulting in the power to take a stand from which point the world could be seen yielding its secrets. The place to stand was the mind, his own reasoning and reflective faculty, which when poised properly was capable of "moving the earth."

Emerson even went so far as to name his next journals "A Place to Stand," and began to reflect upon the importance of this new feeling of power. The first, most basic conclusion he drew from this stance was founded on the understanding that to learn the laws of nature, to understand the human being's place in it, he needed to take a stand as subject, to observe from a position quite separate from the object of examination. Emerson wished to understand the universe, to bring the phenomenal world within his intellectual grasp and ultimate expression, to move the universe with his thought. At a more spiritual level than this distancing from his object of observation was the growing conviction that he took his very existence,

13

his being, in fact, from a source apart from the phenomenal world. This universe, he was to say, was none of his. The December 21, 1823 entry made the following stunning declaration:

> I say to the universe, Mighty one! thou art not my mother; Return to chaos, if thou wilt, I shall still exist. I live. If I owe my being, it is to a destiny greater than thine. Star by star, world by world, system by system, shall be crushed,—but I shall live. (*JMN*, II, p. 190)

This is more than an exultant affirmation of immortality, a statement of faith in a Deity whose reality lay beyond the confines of the stars. Emerson was taking his stand, firmly fixing his place in the spirit and in the formation of the soul— as he would later call his destiny. In less cosmic terms, we might say he had found a place to stand in order to develop his science of the mind, or the Mind of the Mind, or Over-Soul, from which all his later truth would come.

Affirming his independence from the universe of generation and decay was for Emerson his first truly authentic step. His detachment from the surfaces of things, from the gross universe, affirms the material world as illusory, as the Not Me, as he was to say in *Nature*. The essential "Me" or Self was Mind, the subtle substance embodying the laws of a spiritual order, which in turn manifested the reality that is eternal, is God. Emerson took his stand with those whose lives were spent "in the spirit," a phrase which meant for him the perception of a Divine Source and of the life of the mind as an active instrument of that source.

His decision did not mean making a choice between opposing definitions of reality or taking his intellectual stand on the side of the German Transcendentalists with whom he was often too closely associated. He took the obvious risk of being fixed in such company, but his whole life and work were devoted to a much more ancient philosophy of unity and synthesis, of seeing the world as a metaphor of

Spirit. He was finding a way, slowly, to transliterate the language of the Greeks, particularly the Neoplatonists, into his own time and place.

AWAKENING THE SPIRIT

For ten years beginning in 1836, after having traveled abroad and started his new career as a lecturer, Emerson established himself as a serious thinker and able teacher. His message in two major series of essays, his lectures and isolated addresses during this period was always the same: we are capable of life-enhancing knowledge here and now if we can only awaken to its formation. We don't need stacks of books, ancient forms, dogma or habitual patterns of thought. We can have an original relation to the universe, as he said in *Nature*.

For reasons which would become clearer to Emerson, we only barely stay awake to this original and vital relation. The first paragraph of "Experience" makes the problem clearer.

But the Genius which, according to the old belief, stands by the door by which we enter, and gives us the lethe to drink, that we may tell no tales, mixed the cup too strongly, and we cannot shake off the lethargy now at noonday. Sleep lingers all our lifetime about our eyes, as night hovers all day in the boughs of the fir-tree. All things swim and glimmer. Our life is not so much threatened as our perception.

Many times in Emerson's decade of greatest accomplishment he made reference to this lethargy, wondering at its power over us. Why do so many young people fall short of great promise? Why aren't there more moments of creative genius? Indeed, why so few geniuses? How do we relapse into habits after a moment of illumination lights the way to a better, more truthful life? Perception is the door and wakefulness the key to unlocking it. The door leads to truth, meaning, and the authentic life, the great prizes of human spiritual aspiration. As soon, however, as these exalted words sound, we find ourselves stifling a yawn. What is it that happens?

Perhaps, Emerson thought, these prizes are protected by the Genius who guards the door, protected from the abuses of power by the simple expedient of limited energy, a "frugality in nature" as he says, empowered to keep the weak at the gate, out of harm's way. But what are the causes of this so-called "frugality"? Is it a parsimonious nature? It hardly seems so, given the fecundity of growth and reproduction that rules generation. Is the vital signal so weak by intent? If so, whose? It is difficult to conceive that God "intends" such a fundamental weakness in the nature of the creature made in his image. Such dualistic thinking misses the point. The fault lies in ourselves. The beauty and power of the world is so attractive that appetite easily overcomes the gentle rule of the higher will. All esoteric doctrines place the responsibility for such sleep directly with the individual. Forgetfulness and ignorance are the powerful forces of darkness that block the light of truth. As Eliot said among the opening lines of "The Waste Land," "Winter kept us warm, covering / Earth in forgetful snow."

What remains true in the realm of human nature and conduct is the existence of the destructive contentment of ignorance, the easy flow of habit and the temptations of lassitude. The world is too much with us, it is true; getting and spending we lay waste our powers. Indeed Emerson's early devotion to Wordsworth was based on these insights. We dissipate valuable energy just getting there, or anywhere, or just staying put. It is easier to sit than to move. Inertia is a powerful law, as is entropy, which rules natural processes. Things run down and lose their pith and sway. Even in generation the blood thins and vitality is lost. The human stock does not, it seems, increase in force even though it grows in bulk. We are confined, then, by combinations of choice, physiology and circumstance, all operating in natural law.

16

Emerson spoke of these laws in one of his final poems, "Terminus," which reads in part:

> Curse, if thou wilt, thy sires,
> Bad husbands of their fires,
> Who, when they gave thee breath,
> Failed to bequeath
> The needful sinew stark as once,
> The Baresark marrow to thy bones,
> But left a legacy of ebbing veins,
> Inconstant heat and nerveless reins,—
> Amid the muses left thee deaf and dumb,
> Amid the gladiators, halt and numb.

From the point of view of the examined life, then, we need to marshal our energies, choose what we will seek and then attend to the crucial moment of awakening, the self-consciousness that figures so prominently in Emerson's philosophy and in all serious explorations of the meaning of life. Those who aspire are able to see, momentarily at least, the true activity of life: the moving, walking, making of paths, and the passage of days as capable of meaning in a transcendent sense.

We have already spoken of Henry David Thoreau as such an aspirant. He saw men mired in "lives of quiet desperation," resigning themselves to death and sleep. In *Walden* Thoreau clarified the various states of sleep which cause this condition as follows:

The millions are awake enough for physical labor; but only one in a million is awake enough for effective intellectual exertion, only one in a hundred millions to a poetic or divine life. To be awake is to be alive. I have never met a man who was quite awake. How could I have looked him in the face? We must learn to reawaken and keep ourselves awake, not by mechanical aids, but by an infinite expectation of the dawn, which does not forsake us in our soundest sleep. I know of no more encouraging fact than the unquestionable ability of man to elevate his life by a conscious endeavor. (*Walden*, p. 81)

Without assuming any elitist conclusions for the moment about the tiny coterie of those who qualify for a divine life (the current world population suggests the possibility of fifty such souls on the planet now), let us instead see what might be the state of wakefulness required by Thoreau for this enterprise. He says in this brief passage that "a conscious endeavor" is required. The means is expressed as "an infinite expectation of the dawn." All of *Walden* describes and gives testimony to this expectation, and it is worth the time and attention to read (again) this testament to the solitary life. Thoreau's two years, two months and two days in a cabin by the pond's edge on Emerson's land served his brief life well. That he devoted his life to natural history is an indication of the effort he made to conform his highest ideals to the actual workings of nature. He was not one to ask nature to perform more miracles than she showed him every day.

Many aspire to a higher or more fulfilling life, but the seeking is usually only an impulse of the moment, unrealized and not sustained. A vague sense of dissatisfaction arises in many people about the quality and nature of their present lives, but from that dissatisfaction no real sense of specific goal emerges. The *telos* or goal/fulfillment desired remains an inarticulate feeling, and these vague feelings do not find expression in the conscious mind as ideas which can be acted upon or which are capable of guiding our daily experience. The result is that we merely survive, longing inarticulately for freedom from vague feelings of dissatisfaction.

Therefore, it is not enough to know or hear that we are asleep, incapable of sustaining our higher consciousness to a more authentic life. Even Thoreau leaves us doubting our capacities by severely limiting the numbers who achieve exalted states. What are we to do? What are we to read? What learn? What practice?

If Emerson is our example, we need to find those sources which are both rebellious and esoteric in nature. He found such sources in Carlyle, Wordsworth, Coleridge, Goethe, Cudworth, and Swedenborg, to name a few of the most immediate inspirations. He did not find his sources within the establishment of Unitarianism, nor would we suppose he might have. It is typical of time, history and the literary record-keeping that rebellion is tempered and diluted. The rebel of one age becomes the sage in the next. Rejection in one age is the recommendation of the next. Nature absorbs her mutations into normalcy as easily as the flooding stream finds its new bed.

The fate of the esoteric, however, is somewhat different. Seldom in the world of religion has a minority or elitist view taken precedence over a majority one. The Gnostics of the early Christian Church, for example, were isolated eighteen hundred years ago because the significance of their belief was, as Elaine Pagels notes, "that the gnostic becomes a 'disciple of his own mind,' discovering that his own mind 'is the father of truth.'" (*The Gnostic Gospels*, p. 132).

As we shall see, Emerson searched and found those voices who stood alone outside the gates and who established authority within the mind and not within the traditional corridors of power.

2

LIVING IN THE SPIRIT

Matthew Arnold said, "Emerson was a friend and aider of those who would live in the spirit." To "live in the spirit" was the practical business of Transcendentalism in its ascendancy in the 1840s in New England. For Emerson and his spirit-seeking friends, life was a conscious and radical interaction with subtle forces and principles of action and meaning. It also meant a conscious seeking of a reality which lay behind and beyond the surfaces of the manifest world. In a secular world in which the scientific view has all but obliterated other definitions of reality, such a world view is now mixed with other so-called paranormal phenomena and is often discredited as sentimentalism. In science the subtle is merely what has yet to be fixed by experimentation and demonstrable proof. For Emerson "subtle" meant unseen, what had to be intuitively known. It also meant "real" and defined a source of energy by which life was generated and sustained.

Another thing that "living in the spirit" did *not* mean was living religiously, at least in any traditional sense. The Transcendental view rejected the materialistic world in every sense, even to the point of setting aside religion as a material embodiment of faith because it espoused the complete otherness of God and his Kingdom. The dualism inherent in New England Puritan thought dominated even the Unitarian thinking of

Emerson's day. Emerson's instincts were to find a true Unitarianism, a vision of the universe and human life and culture as a whole. Such unity was to be found only in esoteric doctrines, particularly the Eastern variety, and also in the works of Plato and his close followers. It was in Plato that Emerson first found his vision and the path to follow.

The way in which the subtle world of spirit was to be known made Emerson's world view essentially an esoteric one. Although his early years were characterized by traditional values and his early ambitions were within the mainstream of New England life and values, Emerson slowly began to absorb and incorporate into his vision this revolutionary point of view. Shortly after his twenty-second birthday, while still taking aim on the ministry as a life's work, Emerson began his apprenticeship in the esoteric world. Initial steps were hesitant and cautious, but the direction was sure. The first step was a recognition of a basic principle: the moment by moment revision of spiritual knowledge in the light of the revealed laws of the mind. This fundamentally *gnostic* point of view led Emerson to explore those sources whose knowledge seemed to have such a view as a foundation. The works of Plato were for him the major source of this kind of knowledge.

Emerson's early rebellion from traditional authority was evident in the way he kept his journals and notebooks, beginning in his junior year at Harvard. The entries are seldom based on lectures or notes from his college teachers. Rather, they are reflections and observations from within, stressing an inner life of enthusiasms and longings for personal greatness. His most enthusiastic entries are reserved for what we would call today "outside" reading, the unassigned wanderings through books taken from the local libraries and absorbed by a ready and willing mind.

Despite his strong independence and eventual self-reliance, Emerson knew that to enter a world hinted at by Plato, carried forward by Plotinus and the other Neoplatonists, taught by Marsilio Ficino to the Medicis in Florence, translated into

Christian esotericism by the Cambridge Platonists in the seventeenth century, and then carried to America by the work of Thomas Taylor in his classical translations, would require a unique teacher, a transmitter of doctrine and practice. And such a teacher was nowhere to be found in Cambridge, Massachusetts when Emerson took his degree from Harvard in 1821.

The attempts by outsiders—those who have no sense of or sympathy with the esoteric—to draw Emerson away from his radical stance or simply to subsume his work into the mainstream of American intellectual life, have been continuous since his Aunt Mary Moody Emerson sought to save her nephew from the damnation she foresaw when he showed early signs of rebellion. It is remarkable, in fact, that essays such as "Self-Reliance" are so commonly taught in the high schools and colleges of America when the doctrine espoused in the essay is so radical. For example:

> When good is near you, when you have life in yourself, it is not by any known or accustomed way; you shall not discern the foot-prints of any other; you shall not see the face of man; you shall not hear any name;—the way, the thought, the good, shall be wholly strange and new. It shall exclude example and experience.

A few students, independent of mind and adventurous of spirit, will really hear this message and begin to think, to make a conscious effort to understand Emerson and perhaps even to take his message to heart and mind.

There is a problem, however. We face an immediate contradiction in hearing Emerson's admonition while seeking out his message as a teaching. After all, he said, "You shall not hear any name," and that includes his own. How can we hear Emerson and still hear our own inner voice as teacher, if indeed that is what we are to do? The answer lies in the process of learning. Part of the process of esoteric teaching is preparation, a clearing out of the static of mundane existence so that higher principles can be transmitted to the waiting mind.

PREPARATION OF THE MIND

Over the portals of Plato's Academy, where esoteric teaching took place, was written "Those ignorant of geometry may not enter." Plato knew that preparation of the mind under the discipline of geometry (the principles under which the universe was created and is sustained) was needed before more advanced spiritual knowledge could be transmitted. The laws of the mind are reflected in geometric expression, instilled in the mind through discipline and order. The laws of sacred number and geometry were the legacy left to Plato by Pythagoras and were put to use in the academy as a rigorous system of mental training.

Emerson echoed this training in an intuitive way in his study of Euclid and Archimedes. Also, the journals show an early concern with self-discipline as Emerson chastised himself for wasting time and indulging in wasteful fantasies. We in the self-indulgent late twentieth century react to this stern self-criticism by excusing it as excessively Puritan, but it was not. Emerson understood at some level that the mind had to rule the body and the emotional life before the whole man could develop. This small beginning in the esoteric sciences marks Emerson's break with the Unitarian mainstream and signals the beginning of a new movement.

Teachers like Plato, Philo, Plotinus, Ficino, and others of that high level, who founded schools and attempted to formulate the great teachings, passed on the knowledge of their own inspired teachers and took the risk of having the knowledge structured into a system and sundered into limited views. What we now call Platonism is far from being esoteric. It is the petrified knowledge transmitted originally in its purity by Socrates, gathered into a teaching by Plato and then literally sold on the open market of ideas much later by merchants of thought. Plato was very much aware of the dangers of setting the teaching of Socrates into the concrete of a system. In fact, in Epistle VII [1] Plato says that he never wrote down the essential knowledge given to him by his teachers. The dialogues, then, are merely exercises in preparation for learning, the dialectic of instruction. This is why it is so difficult to experience a true moment of learning from merely reading the dialogues.

Finally, all great teachers understand that fundamental knowledge, the only wisdom worth having, comes from insight, realization by the student from within the student. All the great religions connect this knowledge from within with the faculty of memory. The Doctrine of Recollection is central to all great traditions. It is believed by the devout that all children born into the Jewish faith, for example, know the Torah intuitively (Talmud, Nidda, 3). All children born into the Hindu faith know the Vedas intuitively. And Plato affirmed the same principle (*Meno*): namely that of all the virtues wisdom was innate, and all human beings possessed within the soul the knowledge at birth to return to the source of their being. The role of the spiritual teacher, then, is to draw out (from the Latin *educare*) of the obedient student the knowledge already within.

EMERSON AS AN ESOTERIC TEACHER

Emerson was a great and devoted teacher. He took upon himself the task of transmitting in the language of his time and culture the essential spirit of a little known ancient knowledge. His intellectual and spiritual journey, like that of Odysseus before him, began with the challenge of avoiding the rocks of

---

1. There is some evidence that this letter may not be genuine, but rather merely reflective of Plato's attitudes and experience, but it reveals in any case an accurate view of his teaching.

fixed doctrine on the one side and the whirlpools of mysticism on the other, in an effort to chart a clear passage to spiritual knowledge. He was a great teacher because he understood the needs of the students of his age. As a frequent lecturer, he had the advantages of a classroom teacher in observing the immediate effect of his instruction. He learned from his audiences and addressed their needs with developing sensitivity and directness.

At the beginning of his essay "The Fugitive Slave Law," he said, "I do not often speak to public questions;—they are odious and hurtful, and it seems like meddling or leaving your work. I have my own spirits in prison;—spirits in deeper prisons—whom no man visits if I do not." Throughout his long career, he had often been urged to speak out on the compelling social and political questions of his time. His refusal to do so most of the time was reflective of a great dedication to his spiritually imprisoned listeners and readers, his true audience. How could they, he wondered, think clearly about slavery while completely enslaved themselves because they had no idea who they were. First came awareness of mind, then knowledge of the human condition and, finally, action in the world based on this knowledge. Without that sequence, nothing of value could be accomplished.

Emerson dedicated his life to those who were in spiritual and intellectual bondage. From his first public lectures and publication (*Nature*), Emerson undertook this high calling of visitation to the prisons of mind and heart in which we ever find ourselves. He saw human beings confined through error, laziness, fear, poor instruction, blind obedience, to all sorts of habitual conditions, vices, and temptations. At the same time, we long for freedom, looking out from the darkness to glimmers of daylight where the sky and the green hills promise freedom.

The metaphor of the prison works well for our own age. We have our own concentration camps of the mind where we have been confined for seemingly cruel and unjust reasons. Even the image of solitary confinement has its connection to habitual states of mind and heart. The constriction of personal vision and the cultural tendency to narrow possibility to ever more simplistic spheres of power and influence have rendered us unable to rise up and protest our confinement. In America we have such an illusion of personal freedom that we hardly comprehend this spiritual and intellectual confinement. In many ways the politically imprisoned of repressive cultures have a greater sense of freedom out of simple default. The works of Vaclav Havel and Primo Levi in our own time make that point clearly. We in the West live in such material freedom that we shudder at the thought of physical imprisonment, thinking it the worst condition which can be imposed on our existence. But we are quick to surrender our intellectual and spiritual freedom to banal values and religious charlatans.

Just as Plato described the soul (*Psyche*) as being confined in the body during its earthly existence, so Emerson and his company of teachers saw that our highest yearnings as thinking and feeling human beings are held in bondage by a materialistic world view that decries most forms of spiritual expression as fantasy or ignorance. Because Emerson lived and worked in the company of traditional believers, he knew what it was to offend the arbiters of religious taste and the guardians of spiritual expression. When he addressed the graduates of the Harvard Divinity School on July 15, 1838, he had before him the old war gods of Unitarian dogma. Within the hour he had offended all of them by asserting a radical relationship between humanity and God:

> Once man was all; now he is an appendage, a nuisance. And because the indwelling Supreme Spirit cannot be wholly got rid of, the doctrine of it suffers this perversion, that the divine nature is attributed to one or two persons, and denied to all the rest, and denied with fury.
>
> ("Divinity School Address")

27

And fury there was. How dare this young unproven intellect assert such blasphemy? What indwelling Supreme Spirit? How was man ever "all?" The God of the Judeo-Christian tradition was totally "other," separate in nature and essence from the human condition. To believe in God was to believe in this "otherness." Emerson seemed to be suggesting something else.

After the Divinity School address, Emerson's place in the American intellectual and spiritual landscape was defined, although generally misunderstood. The rest of his life was devoted to the explication of the infinitude of the private man. His mode was lecture and essay, his subject was the immediacy of spiritual reality and his vehicle was nature and human culture.

Emerson's understanding of the uses of nature as a vehicle of esoteric spiritual instruction led him to formulate his vision and formalize his method in a manner unique as a teacher. He lectured outside the walls of academe and wrote with a constant reference to nature and society as classroom. At the very least, his students thought they were attending instructive lectures on the conduct of life, a form of high-level inspiration popular in his day. But for those who became true followers and devotees, the lectures and printed essays were a source of personal esoteric instruction, a constant refinement of principle addressed to the problems of daily life, at once firm and freeing, but always direct, uncluttered by casual opinion.

Although he lived *in* the world, he was not a man *of* the world, and those who seek practical instruction on how best to get on in the councils of power and the marketplace need to look elsewhere. And yet there is in the knowledge he sought to transmit the basis of such action as will satisfy the realist well enough. It is the strict materialists who will not find in Emerson anything to support their life-consuming, pleasure-seeking habits.

Emerson approached the role of an esoteric teacher with a proper sense of its difficulties. He expressed on many occasions the difficulty of finding such a teacher for himself and of being such a teacher for others. In "Considerations by the Way," a late essay which summarizes many of the ideas central to his thought while also reflecting his sense of the impossibility of esoteric instruction, he commented that "we doubt we can say anything out of our own experience whereby to help each other." But rather than being a discouraging note, his cautionary reminder is an affirmation of the principle that we learn from the internal resources of our intuition rather than from the directed leading of others. True teachers inspire us into our own memories of law and principle. The practice must arise from our own natural or acquired discipline.

In a letter to his Aunt Mary Moody, written from Rome in 1833, the young Emerson expressed in the clearest terms his (and our) yearning for a true teacher:

> God's greatest gift is a teacher & when will he send me one, full of truth & boundless benevolence & heroic sentiments. I can describe the man, & have done so already in prose and verse. I know the idea well, but where is its real blood warm counterpart.... I may as well set down what our stern experience replies with the tongue of all its days. Son of man, it saith, all giving & receiving is reciprocal; you entertain angels unawares, but they cannot impart more or higher things than you are in a state to receive. But every step of your progress affects the intercourse you hold with all others; elevates its tone, deepens its meaning, sanctifies its spirit, and when time & suffering & selfdenial [sic] shall have transformed and glorified this spotted self, you shall find your fellows also transformed & their faces shall shine upon you with the light of wisdom & the beauty of holiness.
>
> (*Letters*, 1, p.376)

What is universally true, as opposed to what is privately believed, arises from the research we do within the self. It is metaphysical research that Emerson undertook on our behalf. It was and is a search for universal mind, that organ beyond but connected to reason and understanding and capable of expressing through the gifts of language the bliss spoken of by the Buddha when he said, "Profound peace without limit, such is the Teaching I have found."

The first task of arriving at a teaching capable of revealing profound peace is to create the right situation. There is always potential for such transformation to take place in a learning situation. Such is the meaning of the famous Flower Sermon of the Buddha, when he sat before his disciples and students and held up a flower. One of his disciples was enlightened in that moment. Enlightenment is the ultimate in esoteric teaching; it is the transformative moment. The attending consciousness is elevated to a very high level of perception where it beholds the nature of things, the unity within the multiplicity of the manifest universe. In the Teaching practiced by the Buddha such an awareness yields a vision of Unity, the Oneness that is spoken of in the great Eastern texts, the Upanishads and the Bhagavad Gita, the latter of which was Emerson's frequent companion.

THE TASK OF LEARNING

In Emerson's doctrine, the world exists for our instruction. The best advantage to be gained from the teacher-student relation is found in keeping the definitions of each role very broad. A highly conscious mind in any conversation is the teacher of the moment. A colleague or friend with an insight is a teacher. A student or child who speaks with purity and innocence is a teacher. The changing tide or the shifting wind teaches when the conscious mind is attending. Emerson taught again and again that nature was a teacher. It demonstrated laws and "principles that astonish." The world is our school.

If we maintained this broad view, day to day, all day, each day, we would be wise indeed, but circumstances capture us and narrow the view, personalize it falsely to our loss. We occasionally awaken from this state when a true teacher comes forcefully into view, perhaps in the form of a great book, lecture or conversation. In these rare circumstances we prepare ourselves to be taught by letting go of our tendency to be certain about our present state of knowing. We place ourselves hopefully in a place of reception by giving up our certainties. We ask in humility to be taught. When a student asks to be taught, an important shift has taken place. An opening out occurs, a state in which we listen "as if" we knew nothing.

The fictive "as if" is an important trick we play on ourselves in learning, since it is virtually impossible to accept, as did Socrates, that we know nothing at all. By pretending to know nothing, we experience for a moment the true state of learning, and we are able gradually to accept that we virtually know nothing except what we are given to know when we need to know it. What begins as a fiction becomes a reality in practice, and we come to see that we come to know what we need to know when we need to know it.

We also discover that placing ourselves in the learning situation is very difficult. Society has evolved many forms in which learning takes place. We have the lecture, the sermon, the workshop, the school-centered class. We have moving classes called tours, and we have electronic classes called film, television, and radio. We can learn in a car or in a room or in an auditorium. Most often we sit in rows before a teacher who is elevated above us in more ways than one. In these collective situations we are concerned also with those who gather with us, with the other students. Who are they? What is their experience? Are they superior or inferior to me? What is their state of knowledge?

Emerson wrote in his essay "Clubs" that in any formal organization where people gather together to learn, that there are students or members "whom you must keep down if you can." We have all been in a class where there are those who wish to dominate the room. These frustrated souls are seeking a vent. On one occasion, after a lecture, Emerson was approached by

31

one described as an intellectual busybody, and who approached Emerson:

> "Now, Mr. Emerson," he said, "I appreciated much of your lecture , but I should like to speak to you of certain things in it which did not command my assent and approbation." Emerson turned to him, gave him one of his piercing looks, and replied, "Mr. ———, if anything I have spoken this evening met your mood, it is well; if it did not, I must tell you that I never argue on these high questions."
>
> (*Ralph Waldo Emerson*, ed. Bode, p.2)

Emerson put it this way: "There are those who have the instinct of a bat to fly against any lighted candle to put it out." ("Clubs").

Just as there are many environments which may qualify as classrooms, there are also many different definitions of "school." Most of our institutions of learning have buildings, tuitions, hired teachers and requirements for study. Josef Pieper, in his little book *Leisure: The Basis of Culture*, points out that the Latin *scola* and the Greek *skole* both come from a word meaning "leisure," the opposite of daily work. A "school" was a place where a man went (before women were admitted to the process) to acquire the higher values of intellect and culture having nothing, or very little, to do with material survival. It was the old dream of the Liberal Arts, the Trivium of Rhetoric, Grammar and Dialectic (or Philosophy) and the Quadrivium of Arithmetic, Geometry, Astronomy, and Music. The task was spiritual insofar as the knowledge studied was founded on sacred documents and sacred principles. The modern world suffers from the loss of sacred intent in the aim of the Liberal Arts.

Today, long after the death of these principles in the society at large, only a few so-called "Spiritual Schools" exist, and these operate quietly within the culture. They are like monasteries without the trappings of religion, and their students are the monks and nuns of an invisible order. Many have Eastern roots and others manage to find inclusion in standard religious settings. But most are simply places where people of like mind gather to bring some semblance of discipline to spiritual study and practice. The problem with schools, of course, is that they require administration, which often becomes confused with the material they teach. A paralysis of method sets in before long, relieved only by the conscious determination to keep the higher aim in view.

Emerson maintained a strict independence from such schools and orders, but was sought after by them as a teacher and supporter. In nineteenth century America, there were Shakers, Quakers living in community, and the experimental societies like Fruitlands and Brook Farm where those who chose to live in the spirit entered into communal covenants, both financial and personal. Emerson chose to remain fully in the world and elected to marry, raise a family, accept the duties and responsibilities as a husband, father, and citizen. He found a convivial but very demanding vocation as a lecturer in a new world called the Lyceum Circuit, where those who had oratorical skill could command enough audience to make a modest living. Emerson began lecturing in 1833 and continued on the circuit until 1872, a career of nearly forty years.

Teaching for Emerson was a process of describing a moment of arc in the huge circle of knowledge. He told us that the human eye knows a true circle when it sees it to an unerring degree of perfection. A small deviation is seen as a flaw in that perfection. If enough arc is drawn, we are able to intuit the rest of the circle unerringly. The same is true in matters of knowledge. We hear the truth of a statement, even if it is only partial, if we are seeing broadly enough. But to be still enough to see in this way is the challenge we are always facing. We are seldom enough at peace to be able to judge the fundamental soundness of what we hear.

An Emerson essay is one such arc of the great circle which describes the universe and our place in it. Projected in space and time, it rests in a kind of time warp, waiting for the right situation—the approach of a reader with a good eye. In "Compensation," Emerson said, "...happy beyond my expectation if I shall truly draw the smallest arc of this circle." He knew that compensation, or Fate, is part of the great circle of knowledge. The other important arcs are explored in "Spiritual Laws," "The Over-Soul,"—his essay on universal mind, "Circles," and, most completely, his first small book, *Nature*. The more worldly essays, forming the arc of circle closest to the earth, as it were, are "Experience," "History," and "Intellect."

EMERSON'S "SOUL"

The word "soul" applied to human nature needs considerable renovation at this close of the twentieth century. It has gone the way of words like "will" and "rational" that once described a traditional view of human nature. Plato's view was that the human being was essentially mind, will and passions. Aristotle called us the "rational animal." Augustine described us as a union of soul and body. We still speak habitually of "keeping body and soul together." Modern philosophy re-moved soul from the makeup. We are, variously, the tool-using animal, "flesh and blood," a "symbolizing animal," or, perhaps nothing but a history (Ortega y Gasset).

Emerson saw his life and work as a "progress of the soul in matter." Even though secular culture in the second half of this century has stripped the word "soul" of much of its spiritual meaning, in religion and philosophy the word means "the vital principle in the human being." It has, too, a sense of controlling agent or governing center. "Soul" also traditionally means that part of our being and nature which remains unchanged, and modern literature still retains a sense of its potential loss through moral compromise, depravity, or monumental neglect.

Additionally, there has always been the sense of soul as separate from the body, although in the reductionist world of

34

modern science, the conviction is often expressed that body is all there is, that all of the attributes of human life as we experience it can and should be explained and defined as psycho-biological processes, a concept which does not acknowledge any possible separation between the concept of body and the concept of soul. The lack of separation further implies then that when life goes, soul dissipates as well. Science declares that as we close in—if closing in is what we are doing—on the secrets of life itself, we will be able to describe in quantitative terms the so-called "vital principle" in life that up to this point has been expressed by the Anglo-Saxon term "soul," thus fusing it forever with the coming and going of organic existence.

What seems to be the case, however, is that no such reduction to biology will ever be located or discovered and that the nature of what we still call "soul" will always be a matter of speculation. Those who look expansively at life, existence and being will always see, by definition, a wide and deep view. Those who see life only as biology will watch it disappear one day in the limited confines of the petri dish. No so-called "facts" will ever be presented to eliminate or discredit the notion of the soul as that vital principle which defines the "being" part of "human being."

Emerson devoted his life to the notion that this vital principle of the being could and indeed must be developed, or "formed" as he said, in order for individuals to live a meaningful, conscious life. In his lexicon, soul, Reason (capitalized to indicate a higher source), instinct, intuition, even certain uses of "thought" formed a description of the organs of mind relating to higher nature and higher consciousness. The position of "soul" in this hierarchy was supreme, the highest attribute of human existence and perception and the connection within the human being to even higher orders of being, namely God or Universal Being. Jonathan Bishop, in his *Emerson on the Soul* (Harvard, 1964), defines soul in Emerson's thought as "the principle of initiative in life, morals, and mind—the imaginable subject of admirable action" (p. 20). That the philosophic and intellectual traditions find comfort in referring to soul as a principle tells us how elusive the term is.

We have to go back to Pythagoras and Plato to see principle as a substance. In that Greek tradition a law, a number, an idea, a form were all substantial. They existed outside of mind as entities, like a god or, to use the Greek term, a *daemon.* A principle actually existed, like a bird or a cloud or wind— to suggest an increasing degree of insubstantiality in nature. A breath of air exists in a real but limited sense. A principle exists, but may only be seen as application. A soul exists, if only as a way of describing a state of being and a connection to a larger existence.

The clearest definition of soul in Emerson's work is found in "The Over-Soul":

> All goes to show that the soul in man is not an organ, but animates and exercises all the organs; is not a function, like the power of memory, of calculation, of comparison, but uses these as hands and feet; is not a faculty, but a light; is not the intellect or the will, but the master of the intellect and the will; is the background of our being, in which they lie,—an immensity not possessed and that cannot be possessed.

Stated positively rather than negatively, we can say that as Emerson used the term throughout his work, soul is an immense source of power, like light, that animates the faculties and organs of the human being and which is master— one who owns and directs—of both intellect and will.

AUTHENTICITY

In our own time, the definition of "soul" would expand to include the word "authentic" to express the active role of the soul in human life. The word "authentic" has its roots in Greek as a concept of performing an action with one's own hands. It has come into the world of philosophy most recently and strongly in the work of Karl Jaspers, who asserted that human existence consisted of the possibility of waking to authenticity. This theme is expanded in the work of Ortega y Gasset, who also developed the relationship between meaning, life-making, and authenticity. In both cases the theme expressed connects authenticity with process, the conscious attempt to separate the true from the false, or the authentic from the artificial.

In our daily lives, in our work, in our contacts with others, in our artistic, intellectual and practical expression, we seek to be authentic, to say what is to the point, to find the language or form that suits the need and the situation, to do what needs to be done when it needs doing, to say what needs to be said. Artifice is the opposite in speech, action, and thought. When we are artificial we lapse into falsehood out of fear, convenience, laziness, or despair. Artifice is manipulative, intentionally deceptive, and ultimately destructive because it denies the reality of the moment, when what is called for is the absolute recognition of that reality and the opportunity it provides for pure, authentic expression.

When we say that we are living authentically we must mean that we are living consciously, finding in the knowledge of each moment the right word and the right action. By "right" here is meant true rather than correct in the sense of any cultural bias. There will always be those who wish to impose their own sense of rightness onto a situation or condition. In terms of the authentic, however, the "rightness" of the thing is dependent solely on the knowledge which arises in the mind from the conscious moment, which in turn dictates the word or action required.

This exercise of consciousness is by its nature quite detached in feeling. We cannot be emotionally "lost" when we are giving our conscious attention to a moment. When contemporaries of Emerson accused him of coldness, they were expressing their sense of his consciousness in their presence. He did have an extraordinary ability to remain outside the emotional framework or crossfire of situations in which others felt distress. His "cool" reaction to situations could not but attract accusations of indifference. His journal entries, often much later than the event, do show, however, the mark of intense emotional impact which his extraordinary social self-control seldom revealed. Those who wanted more so-called "warmth" from him, such as the ardent Margaret Fuller, were responding to their own desires for intimacy from a man whom they held in high regard philosophically and intellectually.

Emerson's detachment was not only an aspect of personality but also a conscious choice in his life, and it allowed him to master the riot of feelings and thoughts that generally rule our lives. Before we can begin to consider seriously—which means in a spiritual or philosophic sense—how we might live an authentic life in which our soul, or being, is aroused to maintain a position of authority over the riots within, we need to see exactly what causes this chaos and what steps we might take to restore the order which Plato said was our natural birthright.

3

EMERSON AND HIS COMPANY

Standing behind and beside Emerson and his work is a select company of teachers of the spirit. The first of these is Plato, whose work Emerson called "the corner-stone of schools." The essay "Plato; or the Philosopher" is the place to begin a study of Emerson if what is desired is to enter the philosophical door to spiritual knowledge and understanding. As Emerson had it, Plato "stands between the truth and every man's mind"; therefore it is to Plato that we go to penetrate the nature of the search for spiritual truths using the reasoning faculty.

Plato exalted the mind over the heart as the access to divine knowledge. His was not the devotional path. What he taught first was that human beings possessed inherently the gift of wisdom and that the mind properly trained had the capacity to remember a truer nature than ordinary experience ever revealed to the intellect. A passage from the *Phaedrus* establishes the foundation of Plato's definition of this truer, and sublime, nature:

> But when the soul giveth heed with her proper faculty,
> she is at once away and off into that other world of purity,

39

eternity, immortality and things unchanging; and finding there her kindred, she leagueth herself with them (so long as she is true to herself and possesseth herself), when she wandereth no more, but ever in that way and with regard to those things, she remaineth constant, since such they are that she has laid hold of. And this state of the soul is called understanding.

(Thomas Taylor, trans.)

It was from this passage and those similar in content that Emerson found himself in league with Platonic thought. The "understanding" Plato speaks of in this passage is the means by which the human mind receives and assimilates higher knowledge into the waiting intellect.

Emerson was a student of the mind. His experience growing up in Boston, then the home of a growing intellectual center in the midst of a New England religious stronghold, exposed him to new thinking from Europe and new translations of classic texts from England. One such text was the Thomas Taylor translation of the complete works of Plato in five volumes, printed in London in 1804, the year after Emerson was born. It was through Taylor's work that Emerson, beginning with his first serious reading in 1826, was to find his intellectual ground, his place to stand. The Taylor volumes contained exhaustive notes, some of them esoteric in nature, redolent with mystical references and teaching. Emerson was clearly drawn to these notes and took from them almost as much as he did from the dialogues themselves.

For example, central to any discussion of Plato's work is the allegory of the cave from Book VII of *The Republic*. The themes and images of this trope are widely known, and the key to its effect lies in the empathy we feel for the captives chained in grotesque positions and forced to look straight ahead at a wall of shadows, the illusion of a banal reality. The following extract is the passage from Thomas Taylor's translation of *The Republic* describing the painful release of one of the prisoners from his habitual bondage and his subsequent exposure to the light of truth.

With reference then, both to their freedom from these chains, and their cure of this ignorance, consider the nature of it, if such a thing should happen to them, when any one should be loosed and obliged on a sudden to rise up, turn round his neck, and walk and look towards the light; and in doing all these things should be pained, and unable, from the splendours, to behold the things of which he formerly saw the shadows; what do you think he would say, if one should tell him that formerly he had seen trifles, but now, being somewhat nearer to reality, and turned toward what was more real, he saw with more rectitude; and so, pointing out to him each of the things passing along, should question him, and oblige him to tell what it were; do you not think he would be both in doubt, and would deem what he had formerly seen to be more true than what was now pointed out to him?—By far, said he.—And if he should oblige him to look to the light itself, would not he find pain in his eyes, and shun it; and turning to such things as he is able to behold, reckon that these are really more clear than those pointed out?—Just so, replied he.— But if one, said I, should drag him from thence violently through a rough and steep ascent, and never stop till he drew him up to the light of the sun, would he not, whilst he was thus drawn, both be in torment, and be filled with indignation? And after he had even come to the light, having his eyes filled with splendour, he would be able to see none of these things now called true.

Taylor's translation has been embellished from the original Greek. The translator was moved to excesses to direct his readers to the spiritual point. Such was Taylor's passion. The accompanying notes were also written with evident enthusiasm for the Platonic message as Taylor saw it. One such note reads:

41

In the next place, when Plato says that we must conceive a road between the fire and the fettered men, and that the fire from on high illuminates the men bearing utensils, and the fettered men who see nothing but the shadows formed by the fire, it is evident that there is a certain ascent in the cave from a more abject to a more elevated life. By this ascent he signifies the contemplation of dianoetic objects.

Taylor's note reveals nothing particularly insightful until he refers to the "dianoetic objects." In the "General Introduction" to the five volumes Taylor defined dianoetic as "that power of the soul which reasons scientifically, deriving the principles of its reasoning from intellect." It was just this sort of interpretation that Emerson found satisfying to his growing understanding of the nature of the soul. Emerson also knew full well the impact of the moment of release from bondage in the quest for spiritual insight. When he spoke to the young graduates of the Harvard Divinity School in July, 1838, he admonished them to proceed gently in guiding these imprisoned souls.

When you meet one of these men or women, be to them a divine man; be to them thought and virtue; let their timid aspirations find in you a friend; let their trampled instincts be genially tempted out in your atmosphere; let their doubts know that you have doubted, and their wonder feel you have wondered.

(""The Divinity School Address")

The principle which lay at the heart of this image is the Platonic view that the material world, like the shadowed wall in the cave, is an illusion, that behind and above it lies reality. Such is the basis of the term "transcendentalism" as applied to the Emerson circle, and it is the esoteric principle that informs all of their work. It was the Taylor influence during the period 1826 to 1846 that shaped Emerson's vision more than any other, certainly in its outlines if not in its particulars. It was not, in fact, the work of Kant or Goethe at all that gave New England Transcendentalism its particular esoteric cast.

THOMAS TAYLOR

Taylor was of the Emerson stamp: self-styled, self-taught, working independently outside the walls and sanctions of academe. Born in England in 1758 into the working class, Taylor passed an uneventful, yet troubled youth, but one which must have been full of fruitful personal study, for by 1788 the young man was giving lectures on Plato in London at the home of John Flaxman, the sculptor and illustrator. The young William Blake was most probably a guest at these lectures. Later, Taylor was saved from the drudgery of making a living at a series of mundane jobs by enthusiastic patrons, the first of whom, William Merideth, a retired merchant, published his first translations and helped him accumulate an impressive personal library.

Finally set up with an adequate yearly income, Taylor spent his later years translating the Neoplatonists and Persian philosophers. His published works included a dissertation on the Eleusinian and Bacchic Mysteries, the *Works of Plato* (with Sydenham), the *Hymns of Orpheus*, the Pausanias journeys through Greece, the five books of Plotinus, the *Metaphysics* of Aristotle, the Iamblichus *Life of Pythagoras*, the *Chaldean Oracles*, and the fragmentary writings of Porphyry and Proclus. When Taylor died in 1835, Sotheby's sold at auction his two-thousand-volume library, an imposing collection which included most of the esoteric works of Eastern and Western philosophy.

Although Taylor was still alive during Emerson's first trip to England in 1833, the two did not meet, even though Emerson had begun to read Taylor's Plato as early as 1826. During his second journey to England in 1848, Emerson asked scholars he met about Taylor and was amazed that he was not better known and respected. In fact, it was during his second visit with Wordsworth that he asked the old man about Taylor:

> We talked of English national character. I told him, it was not credible that no one in all the country knew anything of Thomas Taylor, the Platonist, whilst in every American library his translations are found. I said, if Plato's *Republic* were published in England as a new book to-day, do you think it would find any readers?—he confessed, it would not; "and yet," he added after a pause, with that complacency which never deserts an Englishman, "and yet we have embodied it all." (*English Traits*, "Personal")

Emerson characterized Wordsworth's reply as complacent, and so it was, but it was also a discouraging note for the idealism of Emerson's hopes for a greater acknowledgment of the Taylor influence. Today it is the Jowett translation that is regarded as the standard in Platonic studies, the second edition of which was finally stripped of its more esoteric content.

In its time the Taylor translation attracted virulent criticism from established scholars, and it was the vehemence of the criticism, particularly from traditional Church of England sources, that isolated Taylor from the intellectual center stage of his day. He became known simply as T. Taylor, the Platonist, a label which meant that he was a devotee and could not be trusted to present Plato "objectively," whatever that might mean, to the scholars of his day. Because he was regarded as a disciple, he had lost the right to call himself a scholar. One needs only to read the Taylor entry in the *Dictionary of National Biography* to taste the flavor of his treatment at the hands of traditional scholarship. Nonetheless, he had his following, and the young American Emerson was an avid reader of his translations, as were many other devotees in America.

What Emerson read in the "General Introduction" to the *Works of Plato* must have inspired him. Speaking of the master's work, Taylor clothed the dialectic in mythical garments and set the stage for the journey of the seeker's soul to its divine source.

"Philosophy," says Hierocles, "is the purification and perfection of human life. It is the purification, indeed, from material irrationality, and the mortal body; but the perfection, in consequence of being the resumption of our proper felicity, and a re-ascent to the divine likeness. To effect these two is the province of Virtue and Truth; the former exterminating the immoderation of the passions; and the latter introducing the divine form to those who are naturally adapted to its reception."

Of philosophy thus defined, which may be compared to a luminous pyramid, terminating in Deity, and having for its basis the rational soul of man and its spontaneous unperverted conceptions—of this philosophy, august, magnificent, and divine, Plato may be justly called the primary leader and hierophant, through whom, like the mystic light in the inmost recesses of some sacred temple, it first shone forth with occult and venerable splendor. It may be truly said of the whole of this philosophy, that it is the greatest good in which man can participate: for it purifies us from the defilements of the passions and assimilates us to Divinity; it confers on us the proper felicity of our nature.

It is important to his argument to understand Taylor's use of the word "felicity," by which he meant the human being's proper *telos*, or goal/fulfillment in life, which is union or, more accurately, reunion with the divine source. Emerson, too, would have been struck by Taylor's description of the human soul as a "spontaneous unperverted conception." As Emerson's philosophy evolved, it would also reflect this dual quality of following an ancient thread of thought to its proper end and of reflecting a new revelation not dependent on any

45

historical precedent. The soul speaks anew in each moment with original expression if the poet in us is obedient to its inspiration.

Both Taylor and Emerson knew that the seeming conflict between tradition and spontaneity was just that, a seeming. Taylor explained Plato's view this way:

> Our soul essentially contains all knowledge, and that whatever knowledge she acquires in the present life, is in reality nothing more than a recovery of what she once possessed. This recovery is very properly called by Plato "reminiscence," not as being attended with actual recollection in the present life, but as being an actual repossession of what the soul had lost through her oblivious union with the body.

The thread of thought which left the Academy in Athens and became almost invisibly woven into the fabric of Western thought was perceived by Emerson and shared with his curious readers. It is a mystery and a miracle of sorts that this thread was picked up at all in the Aristotelian and Pauline tapestry woven by philosophy and religion for the next two thousand years.

The other important ingredient provided by Taylor in the life and thought of the young Emerson was the Englishman's evangelical passion. Taylor did not hesitate to fire the souls of his readers by asserting in fire-breathing style the degenerate state of the world and of English culture in particular. His commentaries on Plotinus, who was himself an evangelist of Platonic thought and the spiritual life, often soared into the upper air of philosophical conviction. Emerson was strongly attracted by Plotinus, particularly to sentences like "For he says, that to perceive intellectually, and to be, are the same thing." The identity of the proper perceptions of the intellectual faculty with being itself gave Emerson confidence that his intellectual pursuits were valid spiritually.

What follows is a footnote, taken from Taylor's translation of Plotinus' works. Despite its didactic style, Taylor's message still speaks to our own condition. The power attributed to material-ism also claims our attention.

With respect to true philosophy, you must be sensible that all modern sects are in a state of barbarous ignorance: for Materialism, and its attendant Sensuality, have darkened the eyes of the *many* with the mists of error; and are continually strengthening their corporeal tie. And can anything more effectively dissipate this increasing gloom than discourses composed by so sublime a genius, pregnant with the most profound conceptions, and everywhere full of intellectual light? Can anything so thoroughly destroy the phantom of false enthusiasm, as establishing the real object of the true? Let us then boldly enlist ourselves under the banners of Plotinus, and, by his assistance, vigorously repel the encroachments of error, plunge her dominions into the abyss of forgetfulness, and disperse the darkness of her baneful night. For, indeed, there never was a period which required so much philosophic exertion; or such vehement contention from the lovers of Truth. On all sides, nothing of philosophy remains but the name, and this is become the subject of the vilest prostitution: since it is not only engrossed by the Naturalist, Chemist, and Anatomist, but is usurped by the Mechanic, in every trifling invention, and made subservient to the lucre of traffic and merchandize. There cannot surely be a greater proof of the degeneracy of the times than so unparalleled a degradation, and so barbarous a perversion of terms. For, the word philosophy, which implies the love of wisdom, is now become the ornament of folly. In the times of its inventor and for many succeeding ages, it was expressive of modesty and worth: in our days, it is the badge of impudence and vain pretensions. It was formerly the symbol of the profound and contemplative genius; it is now the mark of the superficial and unthinking practitioner. It was once reverenced by kings, and clothed in the robes of nobility; it is now (according to its true acceptation) abandoned and despised, and ridiculed by the vilest Plebian. Permit me, then, my friends, to address you in the words of Achilles to Hector:

Rouse, then, your forces, this important hour,
Collect your strength, and call forth all your pow'r.

To stretch a point, Taylor is Emerson's John the Baptist, crying out in the wilderness and providing Emerson with the means to trace the "profound and contemplative genius" from Athens through Europe into England. We see the path in his essay on Plato, in which he names those who claim kinship to the master. First, Emerson names Philo, one of the Alexandrian mystics. Philo Judaeus (ca. 25 B.C.E–45 C.E.) forms the link between Platonic and Mosaic traditions, and his work today is eagerly studied. Then come Plotinus, Porphyry, and Iamblichus, whose *Life of Pythagoras* was eagerly studied by Emerson. We might add thousands of nameless monks who during the Middle Ages inscribed Plato's works for posterity and their own enlightenment at a time when "pagan" authors were officially banned.

Emerson followed his thread forward in time to Florence and Marsilio Ficino, the teacher of the Medicis. In 1471 Ficino received from Egypt the first esoteric documents from the Hermeticum and translated them into Latin for the European community. Then it is woven into Shakespeare ("Hamlet is a pure Platonist."), to Henry More, John Hales (an Oxford cleric), John Smith and Ralph Cudworth, the Cambridge Platonists; to Lord Bacon, Jeremy Taylor and Sydenham, who worked with Thomas Taylor on his translations.

The most interesting, but probably least important, of these Platonists was Smith, a seventeenth-century cleric and scholar whose untimely death silenced one of the loving voices of a time known more for its intolerance and fear in the articulation of religious doctrine. In his Select Discourses (1660) Smith penned a brilliant essay confidently entitled "The True Way or Method of Attaining to Divine Knowledge." It is not an analysis of past philosophy, nor does it state directly its debt to Plato, but the principles are there: the source of spiritual knowledge coming less from ancient texts than from the human soul, Reason as a naked intuition capable of knowing God and as a light illuminating Eternal Reason. These are all Platonic themes and lie at the center of Smith's eloquence.

Were I to define Divinity, I should call it a Divine Life rather than a Divine Science, it being something to be understood by a spiritual sensation rather than by any verbal description; as all things of sense and life are best known by that which bears a just resemblance and analogy with it.

They are not always the best skilled in Divinity who are the most studied in those abstractions which it is sometimes digested into. He that is most practical in divine things has a purest and sincerest knowledge of them and not he who is the most dogmatic.

To seek Divinity merely in books is to seek the living among the dead. We do but in vain seek God thus, where His truth too often is not so much enshrined as entombed. No, seek for God within your own soul. He is best discerned by "an intellectual touch of Him," as Plotinus phrased it.

The soul itself has its sense, just as the body has, and therefore, King David, when he would teach us how to know what the divine goodness is, calls not for speculation but for sensation. "Taste and see how good the Lord is."

It is not the best and truest knowledge of God which is wrought out by the labor and sweat of the brain, but that which is kindled within us by a heavenly warmth in our hearts. As in a natural body, it is the heart that sends up good blood and warm spirits to the head, whereby it is best enabled to its several functions; so that which enables us to

49

know and understand the things of God must be a living principle of holiness within us.

Less interesting, perhaps, than Smith, but more important to Emerson's philosophy was the work of Ralph Cudworth, one of Smith's colleagues at Cambridge.

THE TRUE SYSTEM

As early as 1835, after his return from Europe and during the preparation of *Nature* for publication, Emerson was reading Ralph Cudworth's *The True Intellectual System of the Universe,* a new edition of which had come into Emerson's hands from London in four volumes in 1820. The original had been published in 1678 by Cudworth (1617-1688), one of the more prominent Cambridge Platonists of the seventeenth century. In a late journal entry (VII) in 1845 Emerson lavished praise on Cudworth: "[Cudworth's book] is a magazine of quotations, of extraordinary ethical sentences, the shining summits of ancient philosophy... wonderful revelations...."

It is not difficult to see why Emerson found the *Intellectual System* so attractive. His own researches and the shape of his thinking longed for Reason's penetrating light into the mysteries of existence and being. The following passage defines the hierarchy of mind espoused by the Neoplatonists and was accepted by Emerson and his followers in their work:

> There is unquestionably a scale or ladder of nature, and degrees of perfection and entity, one above another, as of life, sense, and cognition, above dead, senseless, and unthinking matter; of reason and understanding above sense, &c.... Wherefore there were plainly a scale or ladder of entity, the order of things was unquestionably, in way of descent, from higher perfection downward to lower; it being as impossible for a greater perfection to be produced from

50

a lesser, as for something to be caused from nothing. Neither are the steps or degrees of this ladder (either upward or downward) infinite; but as the foot, bottom, or lowest round thereof, is stupid and senseless matter, devoid of all life and understanding; so is the head, top, and summity of it a perfect omnipotent Being, comprehending itself, and all possibilities of things. A perfect understanding Being is the beginning and head of the scale of entity; from whence things gradually descend downward; lower and lower, till they end in senseless matter. Mind is the oldest of all things,—senior to the elements, and the whole corporeal world.

Here, in the language of English philosophy, is the expression of ancient ideas not in translation but in the syntax of Emerson's own culture. Here was mind penetrating matter and sublimating it to the universal purpose and design. Cudworth sat in the master's chair of Christ's College, Cambridge. From this position of authority he spoke in Platonic images and yet found a way into and then through Christian orthodoxy. The passage above is an example of the metaphysics of Cudworth's grand scheme. He also spoke in more existential terms of the path to enlightenment for those who seek re-ascent to the divine source.

Neo-Platonism stresses the ethical and practical techniques of self-improvement. Virtues are considered purifications through which the soul disentangles itself from fleshly lusts. Purifications cannot modify the soul, for it is incapable of being harmed, but they do alter its relation to the body by giving it the upper hand. When the soul gains ascendancy, it appears in its original purity—in its likeness to God. The impediments of the soul are anger, cupidity, lust, pain, fear, gluttony, intemperance and avarice. (Compare the "Seven Deadly Sins" of Christendom.) One should strive for temperance, fortitude, modesty, calmness and divinity of mind. A virtue is an energy of the soul—that is, whatever is good for her according to her nature. Neo-Platonism adopts the four Cardinal Virtues of Platonism: Temperance, Courage, Magnanimity and Prudence.... The world of Nature, therefore, is beautiful and useful in reminding souls of God, but one should flee from the natural lusts of the flesh because that side of one's being is fixed and determined—far from free. One's freedom is found only in the world of Soul—in identifying oneself with one's highest nature. When the soul is inside the body, it is handicapped or preordained; outside of the body it is free. The path of enlightenment has seven degrees, beginning with the purification of oneself through the virtues and ending with *becoming* God. Each soul must progress in its own manner and live according to its own nature.

Cudworth's task in his great *System* was to lay out the principles. Others had to evolve practices or penetrate the principles to reveal the nature of the "seven degrees" and other facets of the path. Emerson took these "shining summits" and "wonderful revelations" and gradually built his own much looser system based on the same sublime view.

THE MYSTIC COMPANY

The idea of the active soul confidently seeking its divine source is characteristic of the Platonic company. Emerson recognized and affirmed the "living principle of holiness within" that inspired his work and allowed him to formulate his own language and vision of revelation. Confusion arises when modern seekers who accept the idea that Divinity resides within, variously interpret how that consciousness communicates itself to our understanding. How do we hear the still, small voice spoken of by Isaiah amid the thunder of the world? If God is within how does he speak and how is the voice to be heard by human ears?

It is within this primary concern for the nature of revelation that Emerson was very careful to choose his company on the journey to self-recovery. Even the figure of Swedenborg, who is mentioned with great respect and affection in *Representative Men* and Emerson's journals, was kept at arm's length on the matter of personal revelation. Emerson would not accept the testimony of those who claimed direct, personal communication from God. In "Swedenborg; Or the Mystic" he addressed the dual need for knowledge and holiness in the search for the truth. "The human mind stands ever in perplexity, demanding intellect, demanding sanctity, impatient equally of each without the other."

We begin to see the dual purpose of Emerson's search for teachers and for enlightened company on the journey. We are known by the company we keep, both in life and in study. Emerson and his company reveal the attempt to balance intellect and sanctity. Without that balance, the human mind swings between these two desires in disturbing cycles. We recognize the face of intellect without sanctity and we recognize the face of sanctity without intellect. If sanctity is void of intellect it becomes dogma. There is no light in it. Light is the image of the intellect. If the intellect is exercised without sanctity, then the light is shown on nothing; it reveals nothingness.

Emerson left the formalities of the Unitarian church because he found in its exercises too little intellectual freedom. It was not merely that he was too intelligent for the "system." He knew that intellect was the talent that had to be openly exercised in the pursuit of truth and wisdom. As to sanctity, it was the path taken by the intellect back to the divine source. As he said, "Yet the instincts presently teach, that the problem of Essence must take precedence of all others, the questions of Whence? and When? and Whither? and the solution of these must be in a life, and not in a book." ("Swedenborg; Or, The Mystic").

The reason that Emerson lectured on *Representative Men* during the 1845-46 winter series and published it in 1850 was to embody the ideals of intellect and sanctity in real lives and not merely in philosophy. He chose historical figures as fragments of Essence. He was unable to deal with the fully enlightened figures (Moses, Buddha, Jesus) because these were too bound in myth and emotion and too far removed from ordinary life to serve as true representatives of the struggle. Rather, he picked those who were, more or less, men of the world: Plato, the Philosopher; Swedenborg, the Mystic; Montaigne, the Skeptic; Shakespeare, the Poet; Napoleon, the Man of the World; and Goethe, the Writer. These figures may not seem now to be as worthy of our attention. No matter. They are simply the bones upon which Emerson hung the flesh of his thought. The present reader is the philosopher, mystic, skeptic, poet, man of action, and writer being examined. It is our own vision that hangs upon these bones of the past. We may recognize in the lives filtered through Emerson's lens something of our own perceptions and struggles.

EASTERN INFLUENCES

"...the grand scriptures, only recently known to Western nations, of the Indian Vedas, the Institutes of Menu, the Puranas, the poems of the Mahabarat and the Ramayana..." were listed in Emerson's "Progress of Culture." It is not surprising that when various translations of the great Hindu, Chinese, and Persian texts became available to a hungry American audience, they would find a serious reading from the Transcendentalists.

The essay on Plato established the connection clearly:

Meanwhile, Plato in Egypt and in Eastern pilgrimages, imbibed the idea of one Deity, in which all things are absorbed. The unity of Asia and the detail of Europe; the infinitude of the Asiatic soul and the defining, result-loving, machine-making, surface-seeking, opera-going Europe,— Plato came to join, and, by contact, to enhance the energy of each. The excellence of Europe and Asia are in his brain. Metaphysics and natural philosophy expressed the genius of Europe; he substructs the religion of Asia, as the base.

Here is intellect and sanctity again, only this time seen as West and East, with Plato as the bridge. The Greeks had extolled the intellect as the proper description of divine nature. Zeus was consciousness itself and Apollo his Word on earth. In speaking of the Greeks and their vision of deity, we do not refer to the commonplace view of the general populace with regard to myth and symbol in the Greek pantheon. That Plato spoke of gods in the plural was part of the process in which he penetrated the illusions of his culture. Plato shared the vision of Unity, the One, which in his teaching became the expression of the Good, the highest aspiration of the intellect and proper home for the soul. That he believed that there were other spiritual entities is consistent with later Judeo-Christian belief.

We learn from Emerson's journals that the Eastern sacred texts, particularly the Bhagavad Gita, were treasured companions, particularly in his leisure hours. He took the Geeta (as he spelled it) with him to the sea when he went away for rests to gather material for essays and lectures. In a journal entry (October, 1848) he says,

> I owed—my friend & I—owed a magnificent day to the Bhagavat Geeta. It was the first of books; it was as if an empire spake to us, nothing small or unworthy but large, serene, consistent, the voice of an old intelligence which in another age & climate had pondered & thus disposed of the same questions which exercise us. Let us not now go back & apply a minute criticism to it, but cherish the venerable oracle.

Here is the perspective of one who knows how to value inspiration from another culture and time. It serves nothing but a parochial arrogance to find fault with such texts, so fine and full of insight are they. To cherish the oracle meant to Emerson a devotion to those principles which arise universally in this ancient text. An example of this universal theme comes from a passage from the Gita which Emerson read when he was a senior at Harvard, working on the Bowdoin prize essay. The Lord Sri Krisna is speaking:

> I am the creation and the dissolution of the whole universe. There is not anything greater than I, and all things hang on me, even as precious gems on a string. I am moisture in the water, light in the sun and moon, invocation in the *Vedas*, sound in the firmament, human nature in mankind, sweet-smelling savour in the earth, glory in the source of light: In all things I am life; and I am zeal in the zealous; and know, O Arjoon! that I am the eternal seed of all nature. I am the understanding of the wise, the glory of the proud, the strength of the strong, free from lust and anger; and in animals I am desire regulated by moral fitness.

What is essential in this passage to Emerson's growing vision is the relation of God, nature and humanity. Even at a young age, Emerson was beginning to feel a close affinity to his natural surroundings and a rejection of the traditional premise that nature was alien to God and to humanity. Seeking answers to the nature of God and the human relation to God, Emerson found in the Eastern texts a confirmation of his own intuitions, and it is in the Gita that the concept emerges.

In the discourse it is said that the great secret of the universe, of life itself, has several characteristics which mark it as a true secret, one worth knowing. Primarily, the secret has to be intuitional, that is capable of being known by anyone wishing to know it. It is *prat-yak-shavag-amam*, or, intelligible clearly before the eyes, plainly understood by anyone. The great secret does not depend upon outside teaching or being revealed by an adept. It requires only the state of heightened wakefulness.

Then, using the allegory of the cave from Plato's *Republic* as an image of illusion and reality, Emerson was able to resolve the seeming contradictions arising from his own traditions by asserting that nature was a sign and a symbol of divinity, a lower order of appearance suggesting the reality at a higher level of perception.

> This belief that the higher uses of the material world are to furnish us types or pictures to express the laws of the mind, is carried to its logical extremes by the Hindoos, who, following Buddha, have made it the central doctrine of their religion that what we call Nature, the external world, has no real existence,—is only phenomenal. Youth, age, property, condition, events, persons,—self, even,—are successive *maias* (deceptions) through which Vishnu mocks and instructs the soul. I think Hindoo books the best gymnastics for the mind, as showing treatment. All European libraries might almost be read without the swing of this gigantic arm being suspected, but these Orientals deal with worlds and pebbles freely.
>
> ("Poetry")

It is at once freedom combined with the intuitive grasp of the way of things that appealed to him. The material world became a classroom where the aims of a high education were taught. The goal of this education was to gain knowledge of and understand the subtle laws of the mind. It was in that way that the Eastern texts helped Emerson to arrive at the intellect as the means by which he would explore the "infinitude of the private man."

THE ISSUE OF INFLUENCE

In a 1974 paper delivered to the English Institute and printed in *Emerson: Prophecy, Metamorphosis, and Influence,* Harold Bloom addressed the difficult matter of influences in relation to Emerson and his work. The issue is this: how is a writer and thinker to arrive at an authentic expression based on the moment of personal reflection without seeing such knowledge through the veil of his influences? Bloom's answer is that "Emerson's inspiration never failed, in part because it never wholly came to him, or if it did then it came mixed with considerable prudence."

Only rarely in history do we find "whole," in the sense of pure, revelation. Such purity is found in holy texts and carries with it the designation of The Word. Bloom is making the point that Emerson needed his influences to measure his inspirations against the weight of revelatory texts. He depended upon the "lustres," as he called them, of Plato, Plotinus, Cudworth, Smith, Coleridge, Swedenborg, i.e., his Company, in which to refine his own expression through theirs, not as a disciple would but as a student might. We misquote our teachers in our zeal to show our dedication to them. That Emerson was a Platonist is clear. That he was a product of the American nineteenth century is just as clear, and in that context Plato is both thousands of years and miles away as influence.

Influence is constant. Bloom's essay and intellectual "presence" is influence. Independent judgment, however, on guard for the excesses of such influence, discriminates as it can, beholding the shape of thought, assessing the needs of others, restraining the desires of ambition, the lures of fame, trying to know the truth in the moment of expression.

To exercise his point Bloom drew attention to a journal passage in which Emerson addressed the conflict of influences while at the same time affirming his own true nature. The entries in question are dated beginning in 1837, the year which begins the decade of Emerson's greatest productivity.

Revealed in these passages are an extraordinary clarity and intellectual energy, suggesting that this question of influences and so-called "personal" revelation was pivotal in his artistic sensibility at the time. He followed these entries a year later with another which expressed the determination to resolve the conflicts he had raised.

The first of these passages reveals as clearly as any Emerson ever wrote the nature of the human condition.

> 26 May. Who shall define to me an individual? I behold with awe & delight many illustrations of the One Universal Mind. I see my being imbedded in it. As a plant in the earth so I grow in God. I am only a form of him. He is the soul of Me. I can even with a mountainous aspiring say, *I am God*, by transferring my *Me* out of the flimsy & unclean precincts of my body, my fortunes, my private will, & meekly retiring upon the holy austerities of the Just and Loving—upon the secret fountains of Nature. That thin and difficult ether, I also can breathe. The mortal lungs & nostrils burst and shrivel, but the soul itself needeth no organs—it is all element and all organ. Yet why not always so? How came the Individual thus armed and impassioned to parricide thus murderously inclined ever to traverse & kill the divine life? Ah wicked Manichee! [purveyor of dualism] Into that dim problem I cannot enter. A believer in Unity, a seer of Unity, I yet behold two. Whilst I feel myself in sympathy with Nature & rejoice with greatly beating heart in the course of Justice & Benevolence overpowering me, I yet find little access to this Me of Me. I fear what shall befall: I am not enough a party to the great order to be tranquil. I hope & I fear; I do not see. At one time I am a Doer. A divine life I create, scenes & persons around & for me, & unfold my thought by a perpetual successive projection. At least I so say, I so feel. But presently I return to the habitual attitude of suffering.
>
> (*JMN*, V, 336-37)

It is, of course, out of this habitual attitude of suffering that we would all climb, like the prisoner in the cave, into the light which Emerson describes as the "thin and difficult ether" of the divine life. The passage shows clearly the Platonic influences on his formulations and the conflict between knowledge of Unity and perceptions of duality. The Eastern formulation of *I am God*, which is most directly stated in the Vedanta tradition, became Emerson's stand from which to form his own divine soul. It is what he meant by the phrase "the infinitude of the private man" and is the basis of his question of defining the Individual.

The entries continue, perhaps the same day, but at least within the next three days at the end of May, exploring further to our benefit more of this exalted nature.

A certain wandering light comes to me which I instantly perceive to be the Cause of Causes. It transcends all proving. It is itself the ground of being; and I see that it is not one & I another, but this is the life of my life. That is one fact, then; that in certain moments I have known that I existed directly from God, and am, as it were, his organ. And in my ultimate consciousness Am He. Then, secondly, the contradictory fact is familiar, that I am a surprised spectator & learner of all my life. This is the habitual posture of the mind,—beholding. But whenever the day dawns, the great day of truth on the soul, it comes with an awful invitation to me to accept it, to blend with its aurora.

Cannot I conceive the Universe without a contradiction?

Why rake up old MSS to find therein a man's soul? You do not look for conversation in a corpse.

(*JMN*, V, 337)

This last comment, after the soaring quality of his affirmation is a comment on influences. The soul resides in Unity, which is the only context in which conversation can take place.

60

Texts are only measurements. In most of our waking moments we are at best spectators and learners, and as such the mind's task is to behold. Direct truth comes from experience "on the soul" as Emerson says. It is an aurora into which we blend; at all other times we watch and learn, wary of influences, but also, at last, eternally grateful for them.

4

THE BEGINNINGS: *NATURE*

Almost the first words Emerson put into public print were revolutionary, but they were presented in such a reasonable form that the implications of his questions seem hardly to have stirred the surface of American letters—initially, at least. In *Nature*, published in 1836, he asked a series of fundamental questions about what it meant to live a spiritually authentic life. Referring to those who in the past had beheld God and nature face to face, he asked, "Why should not we also enjoy an original relation to the universe? Why should not we have a poetry and a philosophy of insight and not of tradition, and a religion by revelation to us, and not a history of theirs?"

Originality, insight and revelation in spiritual matters were his demands, as opposed to stale tradition or the fables of history. There was a vitality in his yearning for the authentic that elevated his search above the rebellions of youth. He had no quarrel per se with the older generation, nor was he staking out new territory in the fervor of American expansionism. He was writing out of a desire to know and to take part in the long tradition of human inquiry. Having grounded himself in the history of his forebears, he sounded his call, and he hoped there would be depth and knowledge in every breath. His instincts took him to the great sources of Western and Eastern thought even while the vital force of his own vision kept him firmly grounded in the present. He understood that no book and no language could contain the substance for authenticity, which was a quality that had its foundation among the living in the moment of reflection on vital questions. He found, however, that the esoteric texts pointed to the way, while not fixing doctrine or establishing systems.

There were in the great questions posed at the beginning of *Nature* declarations of faith and an adherence of intellect to the laws of the universe. Emerson's three questions are revolutionary, at least in the face of the standards of faith and intellect of the time, because "an original relation to the universe" means a personal *gnosis* or knowing-in-the-spirit-of-things, that arises from and then makes active what resides only in sign and symbol in the great philosophical and religious texts of the fathers. A *gnosis* describes a personal experience and knowledge of divine presence. It can be described but not explained, and it cannot be passed on to others except by a re-creation in the moment of the experience of knowing.

Emerson followed his questions immediately with this statement: "Every man's condition is a solution in hieroglyphic to those inquiries he would put." His use of the term "hieroglyphic" had its context in the Egyptian explorations taking place in his time, including the discovery of the famous Rosetta stone, which revealed the meaning of the hieroglyphics as signs of spiritual and cultural truths encoded on the walls of temples and tombs. A hieroglyph was a manifest sign for an invisible fact, just as a human being was a hieroglyphic for a fact of creation and the creative principle which brought humanity into being, which in turn is the esoteric meaning of being made in God's image. That our condition was a hieroglyphic was an added source of knowledge. The idea was to look at the human condition and understand the universe. And when a human being asks a question of the universe, the question itself is a sign of the human condition. Just ask the right question and the answer will be forthcoming. Knock and it shall be opened, where "knock" asks, "May I gain knowledge of this space?"

Therefore, for Emerson and for those who joined his company and for those whose company he sought, the right question made the right answer possible. Confirmation of this first step came in the observation of the fundamental laws—nature as commodity, beauty, language, discipline, Idealism, and Spirit. These were eternal Ideas, not merely categories or metaphors. In this, Emerson was a true Platonist, seeing through the veil of the manifest universe the Ideas which governed its operation. Without a perception of these forms, there would be no insight.

A universe without its revealed forms, or laws, is a universe without meaning, since meaning cannot exist merely in the external, thus limited, condition. If we ask what our role is in the universe, or what the source is of this manifestation we call the universe, then our condition, thought, perception in the moment, all these enframe the solution expressed in symbolic terms. We are our own insight at any given moment. Inquiries become our identity, and are the laws of the universe manifest in our condition, which, in turn, presage the solution to our questioning.

On this same first page of his introduction to transcendent thought, Emerson affirmed the fundamental philosophical task of inquiry: "Undoubtedly we have no questions to ask which are unanswerable." As soon as a question is framed, the solution to it exists as do the means to arrive at an answer. Thus, the only mysteries left are the ones to which there are no questions, which is only to say that we don't know as yet what they are. Space scientists call this the unknown. What we are capable of questioning, we are capable of knowing. Again, to ask is to begin to know. The answers may not always be acceptable to us at any given stage in our quest, but that is a matter of preparation and not of authenticity. Emerson points out the harsh truth:

It is no proof of a man's understanding to be able to confirm whatever he pleases; but to be able to discern that what is true is true, and that what is false is false, this is the mark of intelligence. ("The Over-soul")

In fact, the sword of Emerson's intellect is often so sharp that he cuts us to the quick without our being aware that we have been penetrated. Thus, there is, on the part of some, the illusion that his work is benign, folksy, or merely sentimental. Much of that sense comes from the very real fact that he was kind, never spiteful or destructive. The work is kind in the same sense that a scalpel in the hands of a good surgeon can be said to be kind. Those who contend that the truth must by its nature be mean or pointedly obscure will not be Emersonian. As Thoreau affirmed as well, the truth is sublime, and publishing it for the edification of humanity was a duty and a privilege, one which Emerson pursued to the end of his powers.

SOLITUDE AND HEALTH

Chapter 1 of *Nature* begins with a definition of solitude and its importance to the task of revelation.

To go into solitude, a man needs to retire as much from his chamber as from society. I am not solitary whilst I read and write, though nobody is with me. But if a man would be alone, let him look at the stars.... The stars awaken a certain reverence because though always present, they are always inaccessible.

If we focus our attention on the furthest point in our perceptions, the stars, in order to begin to know solitude, we are permitted to feel reverence. The point is not to look at the stars as would an astronomer, that is, by naming and locating familiar constellations so as to feel oriented in space. The exercise of going alone in the dark of the night to look up at the heavens frees the mind from attachments, and once freed there is a possibility that one might experience the feeling of awe, that emotion essential to reverence.

Second to a condition of solitude in being able to see nature truly is the condition of good health. Emerson's own experience with illness, both his own and his family's, gave him knowledge of how critical it was that a state of good health precede growth in spiritual knowledge. It may seem as if health should be a result rather than a prerequisite, but Emerson was speaking of health in the sense of fitness for the work, much in the same way that we might speak of an athlete's health prior to the race.

The body sends both obvious and subtle signals to indicate the state of health of the whole hierarchy. When the mind is trapped by fantasies and illusions, when the emotional life is overwhelmed by fear and anxiety, the body reacts. There is an intelligence operating there that picks up impulses and then sends warning signals to the nervous system, signals which may or may not be picked up as warnings by the conscious mind. If the response to those signals is limited to relieving only the outward symptoms, then the imbalance continues and the whole structure is thrown off.

When Emerson was dutifully studying to become a minister, his health suffered generally, and his eyes weakened to such an extent that he needed a series of eye operations beginning in 1825, then a trip to the South in 1826-27 to relieve symptoms of consumption, and numerous breaks from Cambridge to rest his rebellious constitution. There is little doubt that these outward signs of physical weakness and deterioration were the result of the presence of tubercular infection inflamed by the tension surrounding his choice of career. In moments of clarity he knew the decision to seek ordination was severely flawed. He even referred to his Ordination Day (March 11, 1829) as his execution day. His oft-quoted letter of acceptance to the

Second Church reveals a fundamental lack of health and not, as some have supposed, a humble weakness in the face of large responsibilities.

> If my own feelings could have been consulted, I should have desired to postpone, at least for several months, my entrance into this solemn office. I do not now approach it with any sanguine confidence in my abilities, or in my prospects. I come to you in weakness, and not in strength.

Had there been some wisdom in the person receiving this letter, there might have been a reconsideration of the appointment. But such expressions of weakness were taken as proper Christian signs of humility and not, as Emerson himself was to see later, an expression of an error in choice of a calling. In a later chapter we will see that the escape from all false ties is the first step to an authentic life.

Of course, some weaknesses in the constitution and some misfortunes of circumstance result in grave illness and death, and when Ellen Tucker Emerson died of tuberculosis in 1831 at the age of nineteen, we see another aspect of ill health at work. The loss of his beloved wife left Emerson in a deep depression, from which it took over a year to recover even a semblance of normal living. Here, too, was illness in another form, the kind of oppression, caused in part by grief and in part by a profound lack of confidence in his own future, that closed off any possibility of penetrating the hard, unyielding surface of things.

Health is harmony in all aspects of the frame of being. The body, mind, and spirit move together to direct the whole towards whatever goal is consciously set and then resolved upon. If the goal is wrongly perceived or is fundamentally without real value, disharmony results and an aspect of the frame of things becomes disjointed, as Shakespeare has it in *Macbeth*. We must establish health first. In health is the assurance that the life is well directed and truthfully lived.

THE TRANSPARENT EYEBALL

It is not surprising, then, that a comment about the importance of health precedes one of Emerson's crucial observations about his own relation to nature. "In good health, the air is a cordial of incredible virtue." He knew what it was to walk out in the cold winter air and feel no congestion in the lungs or hesitation in his step. He knew what it meant to be able to look up into the sky and to know that the clouds covering the stars were not the shadowy warnings of possible blindness. So it was that on a winter evening, "at twilight, under a clouded sky, without having in my thoughts any occurrence of special good fortune," Emerson knew "a perfect exhilaration."

The experience he dared to share with strangers through an open, factual description of what he felt, experienced and knew, is not to be treated solely as a metaphor of a momentary perception of unity in the presence of the cosmos. He was declaring a unity of the experiencing self in nature as a matter of law and design. Man, he was saying, was not a separate, alienated creature on this planet, doomed to loneliness in a nature he didn't create and therefore had to subdue. His true nature was unity.

Emerson continues:

In the woods, too, a man casts off his years, as the snake his slough, and at what period soever of life, is always a child. In the woods is perpetual youth. Within these plantations of God, a decorum and sanctity reign, a perennial festival is dressed, and the guest sees not how he should tire of them in a thousand years. In the woods, we return to reason and faith. There I feel that nothing can befall me in life—no disgrace, no calamity, (leaving me my eyes) which nature cannot repair.

There is no mistaking the conviction that human beings belong in this natural world, leaving behind as they enter the

69

woods the accretions of society even as the snake casts off its skin in season. Here again, the choice of image is no accident. The snake is not our Adamic enemy, tempting us away from sanctity to an inappropriate self-knowledge. Just as the ancient Mayans saw the snake as a symbol of immortality and unity, Emerson sees the same annual sloughing as a return to perpetual youth, where, through the grace of perception, we may return, childlike, to reason and faith.

What occurred next took the experience to a different plane, a transcendental shift. Nowhere else in his work is there a similar observation, at least not in its expression of completeness. It is the religious experience transformed to literature, elevated to poetry and given sanction.

> Standing on the bare ground,—my head bathed by the blithe air, and uplifted into infinite space,—all mean egotism vanishes. I become a transparent eye-ball. I am nothing. I see all. The currents of the Universal Being circulate through me; I am part or particle of God.

The reader is prepared, then, through this transcendental experience to understand the "uses" of nature in a sublime light.

In his journal entry for March 27, 1836, Emerson said,

> Man is an analogist. He cannot help seeing every thing under its relations to all other things & to himself. The most conspicuous example of this habit of his mind is his naming the Deity Father. The delight that man finds in classification is the first index of his destiny. He is to put Nature under his feet by a knowledge of Laws. (*JMN*, V, p. 146)

Nature was such an index of Emerson's destiny. He analogizes and classifies, finding the correspondences in natural events to the order of his conscious mind, which in turn reveals the laws by which the natural events occur. And so we discover a circle of observation, connection, revelation, knowledge, understanding and back to observation again.

Emerson organizes his observations of Nature into seven chapters, as follows: Commodity, Beauty, Language, Discipline, Idealism, Spirit, and Prospects. The first four are the Quadrivium of our education in the world. The final three are the Trivium of education out of the world, our transcendent graduate school. Each category is an aspect of the human organization; therefore, the human microcosm observes the natural macrocosm, brings himself into harmony with the larger entity, and is made whole.

COMMODITY AND BEAUTY

Commodity is, as the term implies, the temporary use of the universe as food for the senses and for the body. Most people see nature as mere use, the resource for survival and the making of wealth. The sun's heat can be transformed into energy which can be owned and sold in the marketplace. The soil nurtures seeds which in turn produce food to be sold and eaten. Emerson moves quickly by this low function of nature by reminding us that we eat in order to work. We do not work in order to eat. In other words, we are not to live as if nature were only commodity.

Nature as Beauty is a more complex matter, since there is the tendency to see the world simply as beautiful and to use the resulting sensations as food for contentment or as inspiration for the artist. The eye sees by virtue of the action of light on surfaces. The biology of the eye, its roundness and receptive qualities, creates perspective and stamps the world with qualities it does not innately possess. Emerson reminds us that beauty is illusory. Those artists who seek to capture the momentary in nature, to preserve a soft light behind the winter trees, may be moved by sentiment rather than true inspiration. A genius paints a vision of nature. An ordinary painter merely copies an effect.

Essential to the notion of nature as Beauty is the element of spirit. Emerson will have human beings, with their reason, will, character and thought, an integral part of nature, which in its essence is spirit. The received tradition, handed down from the church fathers and the Scholastic theologians, particularly Aquinas, saw the concerns of spirit well beyond the capacity of human reason to comprehend them. To the Scholastics, God was Other and as a perfect, complete, indestructible Being is not related to the world. As such, divine laws and natural laws are distinct, related only by God's will in the world. Such is the line of thought and belief that still structures traditional religious doctrine for most people of faith.

What Emerson did, beginning in *Nature*, was to reform those views with a vision which integrated the natural and the human world of thought, feeling, will, and action.

> Every rational creature has all nature for his dowry and estate. It is his, if he will. He may divest himself of it; he may creep into a corner, and abdicate his kingdom, as most men do, but he is entitled to the world by his constitution. In proportion to the energy of his thought and will, he takes up the world into himself.

By "constitution," a word which Emerson used often, is meant "how human beings are constituted." Our nature is constructed of body, "the office where I work," Emerson said; mind, the faculties of imagination, reflection, thought and Reason; and soul, the faculty of intuition or instinct and the natural connection to divinity.

Being "entitled to the world" is a troublesome phrase, having been taken by some as license to use the world as resource without due measure. Superficial readings of Emerson were part of the nineteenth century landscape in America, and the robber barons used Emerson as well as Darwin to justify their ravaging ambitions. These men were not about to "creep into a corner" when the continent beckoned to those with the will to succeed.

This form of blind egotism was as far from Emerson as Thoreau was from being an industrialist, but in some of those corners the errors persist.[1]

LANGUAGE

When Emerson reaches the level of nature as Language he moves out to another circle of meaning. The world is the Logos, the Word made manifest. It exists, at this level, as a symbol of spirit and as an education in the nature of God. Beneath and behind the manifest universe are its laws, few and simple, which both regulate and cause the world to exist. Perception of these laws, knowledge of their working, and integration of their principles into the life form the basis of spiritual knowledge, not the other way round. The study of nature reveals the laws which govern spiritual truths.

The earth is Mother, giving birth, nurturing, sustaining and holding after death. Mountains and the paths that lead to their summits extend our being and transform our ordinary experience. "Who looks upon a river in a meditative hour, and is not reminded of the flux of all things?" Emerson's own Concord River flowed silently through the town, a slow, meandering presence in the lives of the townspeople. He saw it in terms not only of delight but also of insight, yielding in its shape and movement a perception in the mind of "the flux of all things." A river is a slow timepiece, working within the perspective of a human lifetime to demonstrate the beat of generations and ages. It defies clocks and even the sun and

---

1. A student recently asked if Emerson's philosophy was the same as Ayn Rand's. He was under the impression that Self-Reliance in Emersonian terms was essentially egoistic. Where there is no perception of something higher than human will, then Ayn Rand's "self-reliance" produces the Galts of the world, and, unfortunately, those who perceive them as positive.

moon. "This relation between the mind and matter is not fancied by some poet, but stands in the will of God, and so is free to be known by all men." This freedom to perceive universal laws stands as a primary law in Emerson's work. In this sense he rejects the elitist view that esoteric knowledge is confined to adepts. The language of nature is there to be read by anyone. And yet there are difficulties.

It appears to men, or it does not appear. When in fortunate hours we ponder this miracle, the wise man doubts, if, at all other times, he is not blind and deaf;

> ... "can these things be,
> And overcome us like a summer's cloud,
> Without our special wonder?"

for the universe becomes transparent, and the light of higher laws than its own, shines through it.

The passage from *Macbeth* reminds us of the levels of reality we only dream of or cannot perceive at all and of the ignorance we exhibit in their presence. Like Macbeth's, our minds give us glimpses of laws higher than our own which make us pale with fear, and our perceptions often "spoil the pleasure of the time."

Another source in this passage is Plotinus, the Neoplatonist whose works were never far from Emerson's work table. Plotinus wrote, in his *Fifth Annead,* of the relation between mind and matter, which he called the Intellectual Principle, and which when seen and understood leads us to those higher laws which shine through a momentarily transparent universe.

So we are left wondering whence it came, from within or without; and when it has gone, we say, "It was here. Yet no; it was beyond!" But we ought not to question whence; there is no whence, no coming or going in place; now it is seen and now not seen. We must not run after it, but fit ourselves for the vision and then wait tranquilly for its appearance, as the eye waits for the rising of the sun, which in its own time appears above the horizon—out of the ocean, as the poets say—and gives itself to our sight.

The section on language in *Nature* depends on seeing the sun as Plotinus describes it, arising in its own time, in unity, never separate from the eye which perceives its coming. Sometimes we see, sometimes we don't, but the moments of truest perception feed us for a lifetime and guide our knowing. If we are to see what Emerson meant by the symbolism of nature, we need only keep in mind what he calls the fundamental law of criticism: "Every scripture [including Nature] is to be interpreted by the same spirit which gave it forth." This quotation from George Fox, the great Quaker founder and leader, suggests a corollary of that law, namely that whatever level of spirit, intellect or feeling is doing the interpreting will make itself known in the result. It takes a good man to write a good poem. The effect manifests its cause in every detail.

DISCIPLINE

Nature is our school, where we study, exercise, and participate in learning fundamental laws and the rules of life. It is classroom, library and examination room, and from its rigors we receive regular reports. In its classrooms our teachers may be other human beings who have already mastered the fundamentals and who choose to be teachers, or they may be the forms, behaviors, elements, connections, and effects of nature itself.

If, in fact, we regard the great world in which we find ourselves as a classroom like the ones we think we have graduated from, we get a sense right away of the position we take in it. If, for example, we are prepared daily for the experience, if we are attentive and alert to the knowledge to be received, then we are bound to gain from the experience. If, on the other hand, we take the position that the world exists to make unreasonable demands on us, that we would rather be somewhere (anywhere) else, that teachers (like nature) exist only to make our lives miserable, then there is little chance that the experience will have any positive impact at all on our state of being.

Emerson lays out several important principles in this discussion of discipline. The first is that nature's dice are always loaded. There are immutable laws in operation that dictate every cause and every effect. As Einstein said, "God does not play dice with the universe." Despite the appearance of randomness, the evidence of accident, and the fecundity of generation, law operates at every level, even in statistics. This principle challenges modernity's argument that the universe is a great cosmic accident, formed by random processes, and is proceeding by vaguely consistent patterns of random events. The latter is the vision of Samuel Beckett, who said, "What do I know about human destiny? I could tell you more about radishes."

What position we take in this debate is critical to the life we lead. If we suppose that randomness is the law of things, then our lives become attuned to the chaos of events that have no linear causation. We assume the attitude of tragic whimsy, driven by biological and psychological factors to a dubious end, wondering to the last if there is anything more to existence than suffering. In this state even our cells begin to behave randomly. We do what we think.

What Emerson lived and believed was that Reason, the highest capacity of mind, was a sensitive receiver of universal signals of meaning, that once we allow our understanding to inform our reason, we make nature serve our character, which is expressed by the higher aspects of human life, namely philosophy, religion, art, morals, ethics and culture. It is only when human life in its guise as civilization ignores the laws of nature that we fail and fall into chaos. War, repression, depressions, plagues, and revolutions all result from this ignorance or denial of universal law as seen through the workings and symbols of nature.

The second major principle explicated in this section on discipline is the unity of nature, and the importance for us that we are part of that unity. Ours is not a separate journey.

Hence it is, that a rule of one art, or a law of one organization, holds true throughout nature. So intimate is this Unity, that, it is easily seen, it lies under the undermost garment of nature, and betrays its source in universal Spirit. For, it pervades Thought also.

The connection between Spirit and Thought—both capitalized to express their universality—makes the point once again that the human capacity to perceive the laws of nature as knowledge in the quest for Being is the highest event in nature, which in turn makes nature the servant of the perceiver. What we perceive and understand in the actions of planetary motion, in the shifting of continental plates, in the great migrations of birds and mammals, in the society of bees, even in the actions of subatomic particles, informs the human condition. The knowledge gained defines us, describes limits, displays possibilities for change and, perhaps, transformation.

The knowledge must, of course, be accompanied by conscious thought. Without it, we merely accumulate facts and become a biological encyclopedia rather than a reflective being. There is a critical third point in the action of study. The individual as subject (I) observes the object of study (nature) from the point of view of thought (the detached observer).

In a journal entry for October 19, 1839, Emerson wrote, "In the country, the lover of nature dreaming through the wood would never awake to thought if the scream of an eagle, the cries of a crow near his head did not break the continuity." Most of our waking time is spent "dreaming through the wood," lost in reverie, imaginings, false meanings that coincide with our feelings or emotional needs. Being awakened to thought, in Emerson's words, by the scream of an eagle or cry of a crow, puts us in the moment and permits a change in the quality of perception. We have, then, a chance to see.

It is the break in continuity that we seek in the waking moment. That Emerson would refer to the common, dreaming condition as continuity illustrates his awareness of the rarity of these moments of clarity, an awareness he explores in the next section.

IDEALISM

Emerson's overall aim was to raise the level of discussion about human existence and destiny. In that sense he is an idealist, one who asks more of the human condition than is revealed by common hours. His own definition of Idealism is developed in this section around the word Reason, which he saw as the attribute of mind that penetrates the surfaces of things. Reason is the faculty that "tends to relax this despotism of the senses." Unless reason is operating in mind we see only the outlines and surfaces of nature.

> When the eye of Reason opens, to outline and surface are at once added, grace and expression. These proceed from imagination and affection, and abate somewhat of the angular distinctness of objects. If the Reason be stimulated to more earnest vision, outlines and surfaces become transparent, and are no longer seen; causes and spirits are seen through them. The best, the happiest moments of life, are these delicious awakenings of the higher powers, and the reverential withdrawing of nature before its God.

This description of a spiritual experience is of the highest order. The reference to transparency takes us back to the Common where Emerson experienced the full power of Reason, where the outlines and surfaces were not only blurred but obliterated to reveal in the state of unity a glimpse of Reality. This use of the capitalized Reality to describe a world substantially more "real" than what the senses perceive has always been the view of the transcendentalist. Plato's Forms were the "real" basis of the manifest particular. The form or idea of the thing was both its essence and its ultimate nature, or Reality.

Emerson illustrates the point by describing the world of the materialist—the sensual man—and the idealist—or the poet. The first "conforms thoughts to things," while the poet "conforms things to his thoughts." Emerson uses the pronoun "his" in this opposition to make the point of the poet's originality. The thought—Descartes' "I think" comes first, followed by the thing—"therefore, I am."

The best example of the law of the idealist is Shakespeare's peerless poet, Prospero, whose Imagination conjures Reason to cure the ills of his distracted world and re-establish peace and order, not only to his enchanted island, but to civilization as a whole. Emerson chooses several lines from *The Tempest* to illustrate the function of imagination under the command of Reason. Shakespeare describes the state of those who live without Reason as filled with "ignorant fumes" and of nature bereft of Reason existing in a state "foul and muddy."

Emerson clarifies the principle:

> The perception of real affinities between events, (that is to say, of *ideal* affinities, for those only are real,) enables the poet thus to make free with the most imposing forms and phenomena of the world, and to assert the predominance of the soul.

The connection is therefore extended from thought to Imagination to Reason and, finally, to soul. It is a progression within the mind, part of the natural history of the intellect, and it begins with the poet's thought which orders the world to the frame of his inspiration.

SPIRIT AND PROSPECTS

Emerson closes his little book in lyric fashion. His text does not attempt to propose new theological arguments or to promote himself through its pages to a professorship in philosophy. The temptation is always there to employ the intellect in the task of analysis, presenting propositions to a new generation of thinkers. Therefore, when he speaks of God in the context of nature in order to approach the key issue of his task, he moves deliberately away from logic into a realm of inspiration, into Orphism.

It is a step crucial to understanding all of Emerson's work, because for the next thirty years he would be challenged to support his arguments and observations, much to the frustration of the challengers. He would allow his inspirations to stand, just as he had stood, alone and exposed, as it were, to the elements to record as faithfully as he could the laws which arose in mind. It is with this faith, then, that Emerson approached the task of speaking of spirit in nature. "Of that ineffable essence which we call Spirit, he that thinks most, will say least."

The section on Spirit was only six pages long, and it introduced Prospects, the Orphic song of *Nature*. "Whence is matter? and Whereto?" he asks and then answers out of the recesses of his consciousness that Spirit is present to the human soul as a totality of aspects, including wisdom, love, beauty, and power. Spirit creates and is present within each person as the force of life itself, just as we witness the same force in nature. It is through this connection—the life-force evident in nature and humanity—that spirit can be witnessed by the human mind in matter.

The Orphic song in "Prospects" has about it the sound and sense of Plotinus and the other Neoplatonists, who traced their lineage back beyond Plato to Pythagoras and to the legends of Orpheus, before the written record of history. The assertion that humankind was once "permeated and dissolved by spirit" marks another important segment of Emerson's circular view. We have fallen from perfection, from participation in the divine power which created the universe. We have shrunken to a drop of our former omniscience. Such a view runs contrary to evolutionary dogma, its opposite as an explanation of the world. If human beings once stood face-to-face with God in Eden, then the task was to recover that lost relationship. In the light of that fundamental task, the rest is frivolity.

In response to those who later asked of this small book, "where is the systematic argument? where is the proof?" Emerson shrugged his gently sloping shoulders and said, "It is instinct." The attribute of mind that discovers the way back and remembers the path is Instinct or Intuition, and Emerson was prepared to rest his work on that foundation. Emerson's final point, almost a defense of his position, is that "It were a wise inquiry for the closet [that quiet place where we can truly retire] to compare, point by point, especially at remarkable crises in life, our daily history, with the rise and progress of ideas in the mind."

The ordinary progress of our lives is dictated by attitudes, those slants in the mind that color every moment, every event with what we like to think is meaning. What the whole of *Nature* accomplishes is to raise the level of thought out of the morass of attitudes into the clarity of Reason and Instinct, here together in Emerson's philosophy as a single reflection of divinity. Attitudes control everything unless they are released and denied. Most of what goes on in the mind all day is attitude: justifying, demanding, cursing, longing, explaining, rationalizing, and planning moments that need to take place naturally.

In fact almost all thought is in the form of attitudes. We can tell an attitude from an idea in the feelings which attach themselves to it. Attitudes swing our moods from negative to positive, from depression to excitement by turns. An idea is pure, without feeling. We may get excited for a moment or two when an idea arises, but the emotion has nothing to do with the idea itself. Clear thought—detached, observed from above, as it were—clears attitude from the being so that an idea can penetrate to the level of conscious perception. In that light, attitudes can be seen for what they are, false notions of what we are or what life is or may turn out to be. Release from that prison is freedom in its purest state.

The aim of *Nature* was to awaken a generation and to restore what Emerson called "The kingdom of man over nature." He made the point that such a state would not come with observation, as Jesus also said—that is, merely knowing the laws in some detached way—but with action based on a renewal of power. The revolutionary in Emerson would not be satisfied with criticism. He wanted change and saw no point in writing or studying unless change was the profit.

5

THE PROPHETIC VOICE

The first and second series of essays, twenty-one in number, were all written between 1838 and 1844. The depth and range of this work is astounding, not so much in actual bulk, but certainly in terms of its magnitude as vision. As we read the essays we are aware of the debt owed to Emerson's "company," but we are also aware of the originality in thought and language with which this ancient tradition is expressed. What Emerson had written in this period was a new thing in nature.

The initial essays of the first series laid out the essentials of the prophetic vision, to be summarized by "The Over-Soul," perhaps the most esoteric of the essays. His method for the group of twelve was to elaborate on the common themes of history, tradition, justice and religion, but in such a way as to transform them into a vision which was at once universal and yet very personal.

Always, Emerson's desire and intention was to write as he said, "from upper dictation," but he knew that disrupted transmission was the norm and that what most often happened, he said, was that he fell to "copying old musty papers." His occasional discouragement led him to describe his writing in an image from gardening: "... whoever sees my garden, discovers that I must have some other garden." That he felt dissatisfied with the result of his labors was a mark of his standards for inspiration. He knew where the "transmission" had failed him. Nonetheless, these efforts, "loose sallies of the mind," as Water Pater described essay writing, still hold up extremely well to close analysis of structure, theme, and idea.

The primary theme of the first series is the human potential for personal renovation, what Emerson called self-recovery. Rather than simply looking at ourselves and saying, "I am what I am and what you see is what you get," there is a possibility of seeing ourselves in terms of historical renovation, stripping away the accumulations of fate and attitude to find the original beneath. Emerson's vision was an idealistic one, of course, because the being once recovered, he believed, was part of the subtle order of divinity which lay beneath and behind the manifest world.

"HISTORY"

History is the record of the Universal Mind and contains the evidence of our own personal journey. We must pass through the world's "whole cycle of experience" in order to find the basis of our own. Emerson would have us look at the historical record as personal biography and not as the irrelevant actions and events of separate individuals and societies. Only in this existential way is study of the human record on this planet immediate and vital, the way all study should be. What is study, after all, but the interaction of the student's mind and identity with a subject which is an image of that mind? The volume of a sphere and the agony of Hamlet are equal in relevance to this sort of inquiry.

Genius perceives the causes of events and the common forms of diversity. "Genius detects...through all the kingdoms of organized life the eternal unity." The emphasis is upon perception and the latent meaning of things and events. Therefore, the whole purpose of history is to shift our attention from the world as foreign and external to the world as personal and internal. The Greek experience, Emerson tells us, was an expression of idealized youth, a time of innocence and sensory celebration. We can see in Greek art and architecture a fulfillment of earthly longing, an exultant expression of texture, form and light. Standing before the Parthenon, the highest achievement of this era, we are forever young, lifted up and held by a vision that the present degree of physical destruction does not completely obliterate.

The aim, as Emerson writes, is to understand that all the objects of the historical record "live again to the mind, or are *now*." The satisfaction we feel in reading an accurate account of world events or visiting an important site of historical importance lies in the act of penetration, of coming to know the principles behind the event or object. Standing before the Parthenon, for example, we can feel a false sense of wonder in our inability to comprehend how such an object ever came to be, or we can do the studying it takes in order to discover and to finally understand how we, too, are a part of this temple.

The Parthenon began with a circle inscribed from a sacred point in the ancient sanctuary of Athena, goddess of wisdom. The actual temple was generated from the sacred laws of mathematics and geometry, which in turn are identical to the laws of the mind. These laws were later formulated by Plato into a vision of justice and social order. When we perceive these laws, we are able to see ourselves in the temple's oppositions of vertical and horizontal forces, in the human proportions of each column and the drama of each frieze and metope. We, too, were generated from a single point within a sacred space and were elaborated in a complex geometric pattern resulting in proportions exactly identical to this building's.

We may also see ourselves in the human drama of its creation, as thousands of workmen, artisans, sculptors and builders came together under the direction of Phidias to complete in nine short years a monument to wisdom. Behind the construction was the vision of Anaxagoras, also known as *Nous* or mind. His philosophical influence directed the political vision of Pericles, who in turn generated the economic base for the construction. The resulting collective consciousness is what truly built the Parthenon. Seeing in this way, we are able to understand how such a monument came to be, to see it and know it personally, rather than looking at it as an alien object.

The standard, then, of historical writing had to change from what Emerson called the "old chronology of selfishness and pride" to become fully revelatory. This did not mean a change to religious history, but rather a shift in point of view on the part of both writer and reader. As Emerson demonstrated, the history of Columbus reveals not only the routes and dates of exploration, but the height of genius that needed "a planet to shape his course upon."

"SELF-RELIANCE"

"Self-Reliance" is Emerson's personal declaration of independence. Earlier, in "The American Scholar" he had taken the nation's part in its separation from dependence on English culture, but here he expressed strongly, even harshly, his fierce independence of spirit. "I shun father and mother and wife and brother when my genius calls me. I would write on the lintels of the door-post, *Whim.* I hope it is somewhat better than whim at last, but we cannot spend the day in explanation." The key to this assertion is the call of genius, that instinct within, the intuition of revelation that demands to be heard above the noise of daily life and banal responsibility. Emerson knew his task and whom his genius was meant to serve. His assertion of "whim" was never narrowly selfish, never based on a desire to be left alone. He makes that point clear in the same paragraph. "There is a class of persons to whom by all spiritual affinity I am bought and sold; for them I will go to prison if need be." Those are the "spirits in deeper prisons" to whom all his work is addressed. It cannot be ignored that his declaration of independence sounds harsh, especially with regard to charity and the needs of the materially poor. This same section of "Self-Reliance" makes a firm statement about helping—or not helping—the physically needy:

> Then again, do not tell me, as a good man did today, of my obligation to put all poor men in good situations. Are they *my* poor? I tell thee, thou foolish philanthropist, that I grudge the dollar, the dime, the cent I give to such men as do not belong to me and to whom I do not belong. . . your miscellaneous popular charities; the education at college of fools; the building of meeting-houses to the vain end to which many now stand; alms to sots, and the thousand-fold Relief Societies;—though I confess with shame I sometimes succumb and give the dollar; it is a wicked dollar, which by and by I shall have the manhood to withhold.

Emerson belonged to the race of men who had enough spiritual intuition to seek help in that realm of being. He would let illusion take care of illusion and the dead bury the dead. Although his call of self-reliance was for everyone, even those who found themselves weakened by a dependency on charity, what he asked of them was nothing less than the monumental task he asked of himself. His own personal generosity, particularly to those like Bronson Alcott who lived in the spirit, was well known, and yet he saw the need to speak "the rude truth" as he called it.

What Emerson saw in so much of charity was the denial of the primary responsibility for self-recovery before true service can be rendered. When he says, "What *I* must do is all that concerns me," he moves to the heart of his theme. The most difficult task in the life of the mind is to know how one must live. The essential theme of "Self-Reliance" concerns the necessity of arriving finally and firmly at one's own responsibility. Doing a little of this and a little of that, dissipating our portion of genius in satisfying what others suppose is our duty, fritters life away. It is the parable from the New Testament of the maidens with their lamps and oil awaiting the arrival of the bridegroom.

In "The Transcendentalist" Emerson explained that the self-reliant individual had to wait to be called, holding his light in reserve until it was demanded of him by the highest authority. Society looked at this waiting and condemned it as lethargy and irresponsibility. After all, there was work to be done, fields to be plowed, progress to be maintained. The life of the spirit, however, may not demonstrate worldly action worthy of society's approbation.

Once the individual knows what his genius is, however, once called upon to act, prompt and open obedience to that call is crucial. "Life only avails, not the having lived. Power ceases in the instant of repose; it resides in the moment of transition from a past to a new state, in the shooting of the gulf, in the darting to an aim." This Platonic *eros* powers our connection to the divine and has its home in those rare moments when we leap to the new circle of knowing and being. The "new state" has to be a new level of consciousness. The terms "shooting" and "darting" describe the movement which releases such power. It is an energy and not an influence. We experience it; we don't wield it. In fact, if we read Emerson carefully, we discover that the power wields us.

Human beings don't have power, finally. The universe does; it is full of power, flowing, waiting, and accessible. An individual who understands the laws of power can move into its flowing and allow it to wield his instruments. The oriental martial arts may serve to illustrate this proper and enlightened use of power. The master of defense in Kai Quan Do or other similar martial arts, does not develop strength or trickery. He learns instead to deflect and transform the power that comes into his sphere. There is power everywhere for such use, as science has learned, to our peril and our benefit in the twentieth century.

If Emerson was serious when he said, "To be great is to be misunderstood," he could not have been surprised by the misreadings of his work. Followers of Social Darwinism have appropriated isolated sentences from "Self-Reliance" to justify the actions of the robber barons of the nineteenth century and to promote their own excesses. The Self of Emerson, the genius that calls us to a self-reliant life, is discovered in lowly listening at the heart of experience, and access to its calling is an "involuntary perception." Since "The relations of the soul to the divine spirit are so pure that it is profane to seek to interpose helps," we are left with trust as our guide. Before we throw up our hands in frustration, however, Emerson reminds us that trust must ultimately be based on a knowledge of laws.

"COMPENSATION"

Compensation reveals "the present action of the soul of this world." It is a subject of great interest to us because it encompasses the laws of fate, justice, retribution and destiny. Compensation also describes how things work and how much they cost. For example, Emerson defines retribution as "...the universal necessity by which the whole appears wherever a part appears." A crime in the office exposes corruption in the building and decay in the state. No action is isolated; everything is connected. If we want something for ourselves, we alter the true value of the thing sought immediately. When we pick the flower in order to take it home to enjoy it longer, it dies. When we desire to own a painting that belongs in trust to everyone, we overvalue it as a work of art. We pay a terrible price in more ways than one when we want something for ourselves.

The principle of retribution is more than "tit for tat" or "an eye for an eye," as true as those are of one level of compensation. The absence in life of a free lunch on any sphere except the universal one is proven in everyone's education, eventually, and it is in the *cost* of our actions that Emerson takes the principle further and relates it to God and revelation. He says,

"What will you have? quoth God; pay for it and take it." The law of Nature states that we get what we deserve, and deserving is a matter of choice.

It is not hard to understand the law of deserving, particularly at the level of spirit. We reap what we sow. In the contemporary vernacular, what goes around, comes around. What matters is the spirit in which the action takes place. The outward signs are irrelevant, even though they matter to us in the moment. When we assume, like the tradition-bound minister in the essay, that judgment is not executed in this world, we ignore the spiritual reality of our state of being. At the level where we truly live, justice is instant and entire. The murderer dies in spirit the instant his victim dies in life. The gun backfires automatically.

Emerson's experience taught him the lessons of compensation. He lost his father just before his eighth birthday. With that loss came poverty and the hard lessons of dependency on others for the necessities of life, which in its turn generated the self-reliance of his adult life. He worked throughout college, first as errand boy to the president of Harvard, then as a waiter. He suffered from poor health throughout his youth and saw two brothers die of consumption. He lost his first wife, the beautiful Ellen Tucker, after less than two years of marriage. His second marriage saw the loss of his beloved son Waldo at the age of five.

He saw these losses, eventually, as guides or a kind of genius, for the loss "commonly operates revolutions in our way of life, terminates an epoch of infancy or of youth which was waiting to be closed." Spiritually, our losses nurture our capacity for compassion and understanding. We grow in spirit as we are diminished in body, in the connections that appear to define our lives, but in fact only define our boundaries of activity. The loss of a parent, spouse, or child brings us closer to the laws of nature and to the primacy of spirit. The key to the intimacy gained from such loss is found in both acceptance and rectitude.

Neither can it be said, on the other hand, that the gain of rectitude must be bought by any loss. There is no penalty to virtue; no penalty to wisdom; they are proper additions of being. In a virtuous action I properly *am*; in a virtuous act I add to the world; I plant into deserts conquered from Chaos and Nothing and see the darkness receding on the limits of the horizon.

There is in the connotation of "rectitude" an image of straightness, what Emerson called the "erect position." In the ideal philosophy the "proper additions of being" depend on this erect stance, are defined by it. In this sense, a delimiting optimism is the *only* stance possible. However, if the justice of compensation at the hands of nature is perfect, how can we see the evil and injustices of the world in any degree of such perfection?

The perfection lies in the completion of universal action. The presence of ignorance, evil intent, destructive motivation, crimes of passion, all these, initiates actions which end in death and harm to innocence and beauty. Emerson felt that it was a limited concern with destiny to seek personal definitions of fate, to desire to know if we are one of the fortunate ones, or if not, why not. To be somehow "fortunate" must mean that we are beyond the laws of fate, when in fact we are part of nature and are therefore part of its perfection. Nature has its randomness and disorder, promoting life and growth in selective matching among ample resources. The male deer which fails to mate successfully with a female is not unlucky, but merely unmated. The Alpha male mates according to laws.

Emerson struggled with the concept of evil, but rejected it finally as a specific opposing force, in the conviction that the universe was a unity and operated consciously for the benefit of itself. Evil was not natural, that is, part of the natural order. Only man was capable of an evil action, and both ignorance and malevolence were the twin causes. Evil was privation.

There is the fact of the universe and of its laws and of our collective relation to it and them. Emerson always maintained this superior view, not because it was easier or convenient in the face of injustice, but because our true business transcends tragedy even as we are immersed in it.

There may come a time when our race ceases to know or acknowledge the presence of a moral dimension at the level of mind and action. The soul may close itself off from the power of remorse and the discipline of reflection. Consciousness may be eclipsed to primitive levels of awareness, and the species may evolve downwards to the level of the child who responds only to the fear of punishment. There are those, like Emerson, who rebel against this tendency of the race and who still voice the possibilities of self-recovery.

"SPIRITUAL LAWS"

The essay entitled "Spiritual Laws" makes a vital separation between the reality of the soul and the illusions of existence. Of all the essays, this one is the most practical as a guide to opening the intellect to living in the spirit. "The intellectual life may be kept clean and healthful, if man will live the life of nature, and not import into his mind difficulties which are none of his." One state is natural, and the other involves "importing" into the mind what is not natural to its being and function. We might say, in fact, that much of what goes on in the mind is none of our business.

Being conscious of the movements in mind is the key. Such an act of distancing makes possible the observation, made by Emerson, that we have "never made a sacrifice." Without the act of reflection there is little chance that we can ever understand that assertion. How is it that, given all our acts of seeming selflessness and patience and compromise, we have never truly made a sacrifice?

The whole idea of sacrifice comes from an attitude in the mind that life is a drama in which we consciously surrender what *we* want to do in favor of what *some other* wants from us, so that the decision to do what the other wants becomes a sacrifice. The drama comes from the dream of "what I want to do" as opposed to "what is it that needs doing?" If the mind perceives that the cosmos, nature, life in general, and our life in particular are born in chaos and exist in disorder, then we will fill that void with personal desires that have nothing to do with the real order of things, or the Spiritual Laws at the core of nature.

What follows from "Spiritual Laws" may well be the most powerful passage in all of Emerson's work. It possesses such love for the reader and such compassion for the human condition, that we know that Emerson came to its truth from the tribulations of the struggle to find the right path for his own life.

A little consideration of what takes place around us every day would show us that a higher law than that of our will regulates events; that our painful labors are unnecessary and fruitless; that only in our easy, simple, spontaneous action are we strong, and by contenting ourselves with obedience we become divine. Belief and love,—a believing love will relieve us of a vast load of care. O my brothers, God exists. There is a soul at the center of nature and over the will of every man, so that none of us can harm the universe. It has so infused its strong attachment into nature that we prosper when we accept its advice, and when we struggle to wound its creatures our hands are glued to our sides, or they beat their own breasts. The whole course of things goes to teach us faith. We need only obey. There is guidance for each of us, and by lowly listening we shall hear the right word.

The difficult parts of this sound advice come in the idea of obedience and the task of "lowly listening." How can we be obedient to our own intuitive calling, especially when such obedience seems like self-indulgence, or as Emerson called it in "Self-Reliance," Whim? How is it possible to separate the personal desires from the revelations which emerge in some mysterious manner from the heart of nature?

Most human beings demonstrate their self-reliance by being rebellious. To obey suggests a surrender to others, dictation from sources antithetical to our own interests. It seems, at first, that Emerson is being devious. On the one hand he exalts self-reliance, and on the other he calls for obedience and an end to willful election. It is evasive to conclude that his self-reliance is truly God-reliance, which implies, then, an obedience to God's will for us, especially when we turn to others or to traditional texts to tell us what God's will may be. Too often, what we perceive as God's will is an excuse for acting against the will of others and in accordance with our own secret wishes.

Therefore, the honesty of "lowly listening" becomes the key to resolving the seeming contradiction. Solitude, stillness, reflection, judgment, and understanding all come together to guide this most difficult form of attention. In moments of solitude and reflection, arise memories, random thoughts, sensations, articulated feelings, plans, and ideas. Watching these thoughts rise to the smooth surface of our attention allows judgment and understanding to discriminate between and among these bubbles as they burst and ripple the surface. What we accept and what discard begin to form the basis of a humble and accurate quality of attention, or "lowly listening."

We will know that we have *not* found the answers to our quest when we have to resort to *choice*, or willful election, in the search.

> Place yourself in the middle of the stream of power and wisdom which animates all whom it floats, and you are impelled to truth, to right and a perfect contentment.

The natural, flowing power which comes to those who obediently place themselves in the path of such power brings both truth and contentment. How this state is accomplished is measured by an abdication of choice, or, as Emerson advises, "*Do not choose."* We are instructed to follow the dictates of our own constitution, a term which for Emerson meant the attributes of our individuality. Action then becomes a natural expression of character.

We are given talents, tendencies, and characteristics. Much of our constitution is traced to our immediate forebears. Some is traced to our racial heritage and, further back, to our collective human history. We are an inevitable result, as much as a new thing in nature. Even our attitudes have their psycho-biological basis, although we nurture them by habit and ignorance. We are also influenced by nurture, or environment, but not as much as we once thought. As humans, we are remarkably resilient and able to overcome the influences of oppressive environments, once we understand our constitution.

More of the practical process of how we recognize and develop talents within the limits of individual constitution is discussed in Chapter 10, entitled "The Authentic Life." For this part of the discussion, however, the principle Emerson lays out in "Spiritual Laws" shows that individual constitution is a just and natural collection of attributes. By conforming our lives to these attributes we find the right place. By "lowly listening" we discover the right work.

> A man is a method, a progressive arrangement; a selecting principle, gathering his like to him wherever he goes. He takes only his own out of the multiplicity that sweeps and circles round him.

The idea of a "selecting principle" is useful to understand this process. It is as if we are an affinity, an influence; each individual is an expression of forces, gathered together in a particular time and space. We attract to ourselves both what we are and what we need. If we think of someone as unlucky, it suggests that the selecting principle in that person is attracting similar forces, in this case destructive ones. We are not so much clumsy as we are magnets of disorder. When we are successful, on the other hand, working quickly and well to accomplish a stated task, we have attracted the force and power needed to meet the requirements correctly.

The knowledge that arises to solve a problem is simply a conversion of forces in a particular moment. An order in the mind meets an order in nature and something is put right. When we find just the right thing to say in an awkward or difficult moment, it means that the order in the heart and the mind has become conversant with the larger circumstance. A confluence results. When we say something that is fitting, it is just that. The words "fit" exactly because we are a selecting principle; we are a method in nature. It has nothing to do with being smart or clever. We are either here or we are not. If we are present, if we fit, then we speak or act appropriately.

Emerson also implies that there is no effort involved, at least in the traditional sense of "trying." The only effort is to be aware of the true situation, the convergence of forces in time and space and the potential that is always there to arrange and direct those forces correctly. When actors stand in a spotlight, they become a means of reflecting that source of light out into the audience. They do so with word and gesture, deflecting the power they have been given to the end of communicating the intention of the playwright. Such a giving, or deflection of the light, into the darkness of the auditorium accomplishes the great purpose of art: namely, the opening of the heart for the purpose of healing.

If we have ever had the experience of leaving the theatre and dissolving into tears of joy, it is because we have been the recipient of such a gift, when actors, indeed the whole company of actors, designers, playwright and director, have converged to reflect the light of truth-telling into the metaphorical darkness where we sit, waiting. Such an experience is the image of life itself, because we always find ourselves sitting in the darkness waiting for some true light to shower down on us, not from an artificial instrument, which is a metaphor for the truth, but from the compassion and genius of another human being (or god) who gives us his knowledge from the light. That is why, at its best, the theatre is the most direct art form, as Aeschylus and Sophocles discovered twenty-five hundred years ago.

At the close of "Spiritual Laws" Emerson speaks of the "subtle element" which carries this communication. He says, "We are the photometers, we the irritable goldleaf and tinfoil that measure the accumulations of the subtle element." The mind is the receiver of this element; it is the only organ in the instrument capable of sensing these signals from the heart of nature. The whole visible universe is suffused with this subtlety, and the task of human beings is to read these signs and give them expression. Why else do we have hands that draw and feet that dance?

6

BY REVELATION TO US

At the beginning of "The Over-Soul" Emerson reminds us that our most significant moments of insight are all too brief; indeed "our vice is habitual." Since this is so, the tendency is to accept the banal as authentic and the sublime as an illusion, with the result that we forget that self-recovery demands the conscious progression of these significant moments of insight. These moments, however, are essentially mysterious in their nature and are never possible to predict or to characterize. Since "Man is a stream whose source is hidden," the constant challenge is to explore upstream to find the wellsprings of our nature.

"The Over-Soul" is Emerson's celebration of the mystery of the human soul in matter and its mysterious existence as "part and particle" with the eternal One. The image of the "One" or the essential unity of the universe that is the Absolute is a concept which is both Eastern and Neoplatonic. Emerson describes this One as infusing all of life and forming the nature of human nature. It is God *emanating* through-out the universe and concentrating his nature in human consciousness.

Emerson was very cautious about the matter of revelation. His vision made it necessary, however, that revelation be essential to human experience. If it were not, then all religious faith would be dependent upon the past, as reported in the sacred texts and passed down from one cultural group to another, to the end that the essential vitality would be lost forever. This kind of secondary transmission would mean that all revelation was of necessity collective, referring to a people and not to individuals.

On the other hand, Emerson wished to avoid the fanaticism of personalized revelation and was confirmed in his convictions by the excesses of those who claimed to receive specific communications from God. In "Culture" he warned, "Beware of the man who says, 'I am on the eve of a revelation.'" He was first and foremost a spokesman for sanity in matters of spirit. As he said in "Experience," "...it is not what we believe concerning the immortality of the soul, or the like, but *the universal impulse to believe* that is the material circumstance" [italics Emerson's]. Nonetheless, he firmly based his beliefs in self-recovery on the presence in life of revelatory experience, of exaltations of spirit so profound that the mind and heart would be transformed by them. And yet he approached this experience with such caution that his readers might well assume that such moments descended like so many weak particles from distant galaxies, sensed only by those in deep altered states of consciousness. To dispel that sense, Emerson suggested in "The Over-Soul" that legitimate hints of revelation could be commonly experienced.

The evidence of these emanations arrives in consciousness in the signs of a greater nature than can be found in common hours. Human beings are free, of course, to attribute whatever cause they wish to these signs, but Emerson was consistent in seeing them as evidences of the revelations of the Over-Soul. As Emerson saw it, the task was to be present to the moments of revelation, these deepest secrets of nature. He suggested we might experience hints of the reality of the active soul when we are in conversation, revery, remorse, passion, surprise and dreams.

100

THE SPIRIT OF CONVERSATION

In all conversation between two persons tacit reference is made to a third party, to a common nature. That third party or common nature is not social; it is impersonal; is God. And so in groups where debate is earnest, and especially on high questions, the company become aware that the thought rises to an equal level in all bosoms, that all have a spiritual property in what was said, as well as the sayer. They all become wiser than they were. It arches over them like a temple, this unity of thought in which every heart beats with nobler sense of power and duty, and thinks and acts with unusual solemnity. All are conscious of attaining to a higher self-possession. It shines for all.

("The Over-Soul")

Emerson treasured those times in his life when he was able to meet and converse freely with those whose minds and hearts were devoted more to the discovery of the truth than to the accumulation of personal credits for brilliance. The Hedge Group, or as it was sometimes called, the Transcendental Club, was usually such an assembly. Formed in 1836, the group consisted of Dr. Frederick Henry Hedge, Margaret Fuller, George Ripley, Convers Francis, Theodore Parker, Bronson Alcott, James Clarke, and Orestes Brownson. The group was drawn together by a common interest in transcendental ideas, and it gathered with some regularity until 1842.

No one idea or way of thinking especially hinted at revelation in their discussions, but a common level of perception arose in the group which was unique and important to Emerson. There were occasions when conversations truly soared:

In excited conversation we have glimpses of the Universe, hints of power native to the soul, far-darting lights and shadows of an Andes landscape, such as we can hardly attain in lone meditation. Here are oracles sometimes

101

profusely given, to which the memory goes back in barren hours. ("The Over-Soul")

Emerson was by natural inclination and conscious intent reticent in these conversations. His role seemed to have been to offer both an elevated presence against which others could measure their own contribution and a silence within which observation could truly be heard. His relative silence was never critical, however, as was that of Thoreau, who would often retire from a conversational group when he felt it no longer worthy of his higher aims. Emerson, on the other hand, was immensely patient as a listener. He quietly kept the room in view and made the relevant comment or the keen observation that kept the conversation progressing at an elevated level.

In "Inspiration," from *Letters and Social Aims,* he said of the powers of conversation:

Conversation... is the right metaphysical professor. This is the true school of philosophy,—this the college where you learn what thoughts are, what powers lurk in those fugitive gleams, and what becomes of them; how they make history.

He then qualified the role of conversation somewhat by affirming that the best perceptions "are granted to the single soul," but in conversation "a principle appears to all: we see new relations, many truths; every mind seizes them as they pass." ("Inspiration"). Therefore, conversation offered the first hint of revelation, insofar as broad principles surfaced which helped to frame more personal experiences.

REVERY AS DISCIPLINE

By revery Emerson meant recollection or to collect again or to recover the significant past, particularly the purity and innocence of youth. He did not mean pouring over yesterday's events to make the memory of them more palatable, i.e., justification and rationalization. Revery meant bringing to mind again what had been lost. It hints at the principle that our own personal history, well recollected, is a sign, or a hieroglyphic, of universal laws and our personal connection to them.

Most of us never suppose that what we remember from childhood has any relevance to our search for higher knowledge. Certain memories, however, remain in the mind and seem to arise in moments of crisis or in moments of peace and contentment. Some conscious attention to these moments, actually watching these memories as they arise, may offer knowledge of how we see our experience and what life-forming images influence our actions and attitudes.

By their nature, reveries are personal. They evoke images of specific experience in time and place. Emerson struggled with this contradiction and finally realized that we could not avoid filtering what might be universal through the individual instrument. In "Experience" he said,

> And we cannot say too little of our constitutional necessity of seeing things under private aspects, or saturated with our humors. And yet is the God the native of these bleak rocks. That need makes in morals the capital virtue of self-trust. We must hold hard to this poverty, however scandalous, and by more vigorous self-recoveries, after the sallies of action, possess our axis more firmly.

Here we see Emerson being extremely cautious, exploring with his most evasive language the reality of this experience. His position seems to be that God, the Over-Soul, is the natural ground of revery—as opposed to fanciful imagination or illusion—and that in this desert (this poverty) the waters of revelation are indeed scarce. He even excuses what he calls the scandalous nature of the claim for something higher and offers the test of action and rigorous scrutiny in our efforts at self-recovery.

There is ample reason to be confused about the difference between the word revery and the mental state that Emerson calls fancy. In "Experience" he said,

> Men live in their fancy, like drunkards whose hands are too soft and tremulous for successful labor. It is a tempest of fancies, and the only ballast I know, is a respect to the present hour.

Fancy is uncontrolled, unconscious mental drifting, the kind that occupies the mind much of the day and is typified by daydreaming. The sort of revery that leads to the possibility of revelation must, therefore, be a conscious, reflective discipline of mind. Another term for it might be self-remembering. As Emerson said later on in "Experience," "The line he must walk is a hair's breadth."

REMORSE AND HUMAN WILL

Emerson next refers to remorse as a hint of revelation. The first step in understanding the relationship of remorse to revelation is to separate it from the muddy waters of guilt. Remorse is a recognition of wrong action experienced as feeling. It is a recognition powered by the love of truth, and it results in reconciliation when the feeling is openly acknowledged and acted upon. Just how Emerson related remorse to revelation is revealed in a passage from the "Divinity School Address":

> The sentiment of virtue is a reverence and delight in the presence of certain divine laws. It perceives that this homely game of life we play, covers, under what seems foolish details, principles that astonish. The child amidst

his baubles is learning the action of light, motion, gravity, muscular force; and in the game of human life, love, fear, justice, appetite, man, and God, interact. These laws refuse to be adequately stated. They will not be written out on paper, or spoken by the tongue. They elude our persevering thought; yet we read them hourly in each other's faces, in each other's actions, in our own remorse.... Thus in the soul of man there is a justice whose retributions are instant and entire. The heart which abandons itself to the Supreme mind finds itself related to all its works, and will travel a royal road to particular knowledges and powers.

It is the power of remorse working itself out in the crucible of conscious reflection that produces this knowledge and power. To obey the dictates of the heart makes accessible the Supreme Mind and all of its gifts. The remorse experienced in hurting another or disobeying moral standards begins in the silence of suffering. We hold on to the knowledge of wrongdoing until we begin to experience the effects of denial and the refusal to correct the wrong. Slowly, the workings of remorse begin to show the way to repentance and there is joy in finding the courage to make amends.

An example of the power of personal revery and the pangs of remorse appears in Emerson's journal for March, 1838. The occasion was a discussion with his second wife Lidian (as he called her) as he reflected on memories of his first wife, Ellen Tucker Emerson, and his two deceased brothers, Charles and Edward.

Last night a remembering & remembering talk with Lidian. I went back to the first smile of Ellen on the door stone at Concord. I went back to all that delicious relation to feel as ever how many shades, how much reproach. Strange is it that I can go back to no part of youth, no past relation without shrinking & shrinking. Not Ellen, not

Edward, not Charles. Infinite compunctions embitter each of those dear names & all who surround them. Ah could I have felt in the presence of the first, as now I feel my own power and hope, & so have offered her in every word & look the heart of a man humble & wise, but resolved to be true & perfect with God, & not as I fear it seemed, the uneasy uncentred joy of one who received in her a good—a lovely good—out of all proportion to his deserts, I might haply have made her days longer & certainly sweeter & at least have recalled her seraph smile without a pang. . . . Well O God I will try & learn, from this sad memory to be brave & circumspect & true henceforth & weave now a web that will not shrink.

(*JMN,* V, p. 456)

Another aspect of remorse is its relation to will and the degree of freedom we attach to it. Henry James characterized human beings as having what he called the "judgment of regret." The existence of this judgment, he argued, meant that the actions of human beings were not predetermined. We are not machines, destined to act in a certain way, driven by mechanistic forces. If a human being is capable of feeling remorse, it means that choice exists as a faculty of the mind. How can we regret an action which is out of our power to control?

THE PASSION TO PROCEED

Passion is the torch that guides us on the royal road to higher knowledge. Emerson's definition of passion comes close to Plato's use of the term *eros.* It is the power by which revelation travels the distance from divinity to the mortal soul, like a spark jumping between two electrodes. Without this passion there is no bridging of the gap, no communication across the subtle space.

Passion, though a bad regulator, is a powerful spring....
'Tis the heat which sets our human atoms spinning,
overcomes the friction of crossing thresholds and first
addresses in society, and gives us a good start and speed,
easy to continue when once it is begun."

("Considerations By The Way")

Emerson realized the strength of inertia, the unwillingness
to start down the road, to express what one knew, to open
the heart to the search for truth. It is easier to remain silent,
to hide the light and avoid the attacks and jibes of society. But
passion is not only necessary as a spring; it is also liberating
as a source of revelation. To make the public address, to
cross the threshold into society, is to understand as well as to
obey. And like the laws of inertia, it is easier to keep going
once the forward motion has begun.

Emerson's own early experience gave him the insight to
connect passion to revelation. Although his personal
demeanor was cool—some said downright cold—Emerson
displayed his passion in overcoming barriers to his own development. After leaving the ministry, which would have been
for him a safe and secure profession for life, he faced an
uncertain future. In 1833, back from his European odyssey,
he determined to begin lecturing. With no organization to
support him, with no firm expertise to market himself, he
organized his first lecture series, hired the hall, sold the
tickets, and gave his first lectures to modest but growing
audiences.

Without the passion of his convictions, his "place to
stand," he would not have overcome the inertia of the professional stagnation facing him after the death of Ellen and
the loss of a safe profession. Enthusiasm, the power of being
en theos or "with the god," carried him across the threshold,
opened the doors, and gave him his first audiences. That he
connects this value to revelation is consistent with his view
of life itself as an experience in self-recovery.

SURPRISE

By including surprise as an element in the transmittal of spiritual knowledge, Emerson recognizes that true discovery is always made obliquely and never as a result of expectation of a particular result. Often what gets in the way of revelation is the expectation of discovery, the thought that we know what it is that we hope to uncover in the search. How could we anticipate the nature and content of an insight from a source we don't even know and don't understand? Such a result would have to be a self-fulfilling prophecy. The element of surprise guarantees, at least, that expectation of an experience wasn't the catalyst.

> I prefer to say with the old prophet, "Seekest thou great things? Seek them not." Life is a boundless privilege, and when you pay for your ticket and get into the car [as in train], you have no guess what good company you shall find there. You buy much that is not rendered in the bill. Men achieve a certain greatness unawares, when working to another aim....Nature does not like to be observed, and likes that we should be her fools and playmates. We may have the sphere [planet] for our cricket-ball, but not a berry for our philosophy. Direct strokes she never gave us the power to make; all our blows glance, all our hits are accidents. ("Experience")

Emerson knew well how rare such moments were and how oddly in time and place they appeared. His "transparent eyeball" experience happened at twilight on an otherwise uneventful evening, when the Common was dotted with snow puddles, as opposed to shafts of spiritual sunlight, and when no particular thought or feeling of special significance filled his mind. Indeed, the conscious desire to have such an experience actually seems to prevent its occurrence. The conscious mind must be caught at rest, momentarily off guard, so that the gates of reception are open. Thus, the passion to know must not be directed to false ideas about what is to be known.

In "Circles," from the first series of essays, Emerson relates surprise to the business of "building up our being," and he affirms the principle that higher knowledge must by definition come in the form of a surprise.

> Life is a series of surprises. We do not guess to-day the mood, the pleasure, the power of tomorrow, when we are building up our being. Of lower states,—of acts of routine and sense,—we can tell somewhat; but the masterpieces of God, the total growths and universal movements of the soul, he hideth; they are incalculable. I can know that truth is divine and helpful; but how it shall help me I can have no guess, for *so to be* is the sole inlet of *so to know.*

This last sentence, the relation between being and knowing, is elusive, at least in its expression, but it is crucial in understanding Emerson's sense of revelation in relation to the individual life. In effect, we can know only what our state of being tells us, both in terms of intellect and situation. *So,* in the sense of *thus* and also *then,* suggesting moment and immediacy, directs the attention to *being,* the very moment of perception. This strong direction from Emerson, the way he employs the language to direct attention, affirms the role of surprise in *how* we know *what* we know. "Sole inlet" closes off any means of *gnosis* other than the moment of being.

THE WORLD OF DREAMS

In the great esoteric traditions, dreams often play an important oracular role. Emerson pursued the subject, however, with care and was very circumspect in writing about it. The rare descriptions of his own dreams appear only in the journals and show an awareness of the dark side of the human personality,

109

as well as the absurd and often whimsical side. The occasional glimpses of the function of dreams in revelation show Emerson's awareness of the role dreams play in providing access to primary truth:

> We are led by this experience into the high region of Cause, and acquainted with the identity of very unlike-seeming effects. We learn that actions whose turpitude is very differently reputed proceed from one and the same affection. Sleep takes off the costume of circumstance, arms us with terrible freedom, so that every will rushes to a deed. A skilful man reads his dreams for his self-knowledge; yet not the details, but the quality. What part does he play in them,—a cheerful, manly part, or a poor drivelling part? However monstrous and grotesque their apparitions, they have a substantial truth. ("Demonology")

The presence of a nightmare signals an oppressive state of mind which only reflection can uncover. We ignore such signals at our peril. A dream is a sign along the road. Reading it and either proceeding or changing direction is as important to living consciously as reading the roadsign is to traveling successfully.

In a journal entry dated October 25, 1840, Emerson wrote:

> I dreamed that I floated at will in the great ether, and I saw this world floating also not far off, but diminished to the size of an apple. Then an angel took it in his hand and brought it to me and said, "This thou must eat." And I ate the world.

This dream, first, is an image of the stand outside the self. He is floating *at will* in space, free to move anywhere. The distancing gives Emerson the power to "eat the world," putting it at his service as food for the soul. The angel, the higher self within, commands the traveler to eat, to transform the apple/world and himself. It is necessary, of course, for the self to be in a position suitable for such a command. The stance above the world invites the next step. Obedience to the command permits the transformation.

Dreams lead us into knowledge, in fact "may let us deeper into the secret of nature than a hundred concerted experiments" (*Nature*, "Prospects"). Emerson explains that view more fully in a full passage from "Demonology" (1838-39), an essay often quoted in part but seldom published entire. The reading public saw it for the first time in 1877. Since the essay is hard to come by, the passage is printed here at length.

> Dreams have a poetic integrity and truth. This limbo and dust-hole of thought is presided over by a certain reason, too. Their extravagance from nature is yet within a higher nature. They seem to us to suggest an abundance and fluency of thought not familiar to the waking experience. They pique us by independence of us, yet we know ourselves in this mad crowd, and we owe to dreams a kind of divination and wisdom. My dreams are not me; they are not Nature, or the Not-me: they are both. They have a double consciousness, at once sub- and ob-jective. We call the phantoms that rise, the creation of our fancy, but they act like mutineers, and fire on their commander; showing that every act, every thought, every cause, is bipolar, and in the act is contained the counteraction. If I strike, I am struck; if I chase, I am pursued.
>
> Wise and sometimes terrible hints shall in them be thrown to the man out of a quite unknown intelligence. He shall be startled two or three times in his life by the justice as well as the significance of this phantasmagoria. Once or twice the conscious fetters shall seem to be unlocked, and a freer utterance attained. A prophetic character in all ages has haunted them. They are the maturation often of opinions carried out to statements, but whereof we already possessed the elements. Thus, when awake, I know the

character of Rupert, but do not think what he may do. In dreams I see him engaged in certain actions which seem preposterous,—out of all fitness. He is hostile, he is cruel, he is frightful, he is a poltroon. It turns out prophecy a year later. But it was already in my mind as character, and the sibyl dreams merely embodied it in fact. Why then should not symptoms, auguries, forebodings be, and, as one said, the moanings of the spirit? ....A skillful man reads his dreams for his self-knowledge; yet not the details, but the quality.

The element of discipline enters into this scene as well. To be able to watch the dream, to see it as an aspect of the mind at play or in suffering, allows us to keep these fantasies in place. Repression is neither useful nor possible. Thinking of dreams as separate entirely from our experience and our character is foolish because it is dishonest and probably dangerous. Thinking of dreams as a literal expression of our true nature is foolish and even more dangerous because we may believe a dream is a literal instruction. As Emerson so carefully says, "A skilful man reads his dreams for his self-knowledge." The rest is illusion.

THE CONTENT OF REVELATION

Emerson devotes ample space in "The Over-Soul" to the content of revelation. His method is to discuss what revelation does *not* reveal and then what it does, or at least what its laws are. He says first, "Before the revelations of the soul, Time, Space and Nature shrink away." Little seems to be left, and we may wonder what of human relevance revelation can address? Our experience is in time, space, and nature, making it difficult to accept or understand knowledge outside these realms. Our natural desire is to know when, where, and how our lives will progress. Emerson spoke of the soul as having "no dates, nor rites, nor persons, nor specialties, nor men. The soul knows only the soul" ("The Over-Soul").

The human task, then, is to know the soul and not ask the soul to know us. Again, the conscious mind is in charge when we ask for divine guidance in our jobs or in our relationships and is even more involved when we expect an answer like "Quit tomorrow!". The soul, as Emerson said, is not concerned with Tuesday, New York, or personal biographies. The soul knows only itself.

> We know the truth when we see it, let skeptic and scoffer say what they choose. Foolish people ask you, when you have spoken what they do not wish to hear, "How do you know it is the truth, and not an error of your own?" We know the truth when we see it, from opinion, as we know when we are awake that we are awake. ("The Over-Soul")

Emerson knew more than he was willing to reveal in making such a statement, however. Most people are asleep most of the time. We know well enough that the waking state in which the voice of the soul is heard is all too rare, and rarer still is the awakened eye of one who is reflecting its truth. Emerson knew that we often affirm to be true what most pleases us at the time. One of the first tasks of discernment is to remove the pleasure principle from the arena. What is true has nothing to do with what is pleasant, or unpleasant for that matter. Personal pleasure is simply not involved. What is involved is the law. Emerson constantly made that connection.

He says in many places throughout the essays that the nature of revelation is the same as perception of the law, and that the *expression* of the law is the same as nature—the physical universe. Thus, our task as human beings is to be perceivers of universal law. That is what we do. It is our purpose. Ours is to know the Divine Thought. It is a gift, a destiny, and a responsibility. With it, he said, come great and sudden enlargements of power.

Emerson devoted space in "Spiritual Laws" to correcting the assumption that somehow universal law has nothing to do with us. It is reassuring to know that although the Over-Soul is a universal element, there is a profound way in which the individual constitution (or essence of the individual) relates correctly and specifically to spiritual laws.

Emerson defined heaven as that state in which the individual existed on earth doing the right work according to universal law.

> Each man has his own vocation. The talent is the call. There is one direction in which all space is open to him. He has faculties silently inviting him thither to endless exertion. He is like a ship in a river; he runs against obstructions on every side but one, on that side all obstruction is taken away and he sweeps serenely over a deepening channel into an infinite sea. ("Spiritual Laws")

This theme and the imagery which explains it demonstrate how perception of the law is both natural and liberating. We need only understand the direction in which all space is open to us. That task, however, can be the most difficult in life. There are so many ideas and opinions about where talents lie and where the opportunities are to develop them. Much of this theme will be seen in the next chapter, devoted to the escape from false ties, since escape is often the first step in understanding what we are to do with our lives. It is tragic that so many people suffer all their lives under false notions and live their lives bound by the opinions and desires of others.

Emerson affirms most clearly and well the great laws of revelation and the role we play in receiving them and finding the way to give expresssion of them to others.

> The revelation of Thought takes man out of servitude into freedom. We rightly say of ourselves, we were born and afterward we were born again, and many times. We have

successive experiences so important that the new forgets the old, and hence the mythology of the seven or the nine heavens. The day of days, the great day of the feast of life, is that in which the inward eye opens to the Unity of things, to the omnipresence of law: sees that what is, must be, and ought to be, or is the best. This beatitude dips from on high down on us and we see. It is not in us so much as we are in it. If the air come to our lungs, we breathe and live; if not, we die. If the light come to our eyes, we see; else not. And if truth comes to our mind, we suddenly expand to its dimensions, as if we grew to worlds. We are as lawgivers; we seek for Nature; we prophesy and divine. ("Fate")

That we are in this Unity rather than it being within us is crucial to the attitude we may have of our relationship to the divine. Expanding to its dimensions allows us to participate in the larger reality while knowing, in those moments, how much broader and deeper our experience can be.

There is a danger inherent in any consideration of the content of revelation, that we will be tempted into what Emerson called a "low curiosity and lust of structure." It is true that we lust after knowledge of the hereafter and are drawn to claims in the realm of spiritual phenomena. As Emerson wrote in "Demonology," we are exposed during a lifetime to enough hints of extraordinary events and glimpses into the so-called "beyond" to make us susceptible to charlatans and madmen. It would be saner to regard such glimpses as small hints of a greater reality to which we might someday have a wiser understanding. Emerson warned in "Demonology":

Animal magnetism, omens, spiritism, mesmerism have great interest for some minds. They run into this twilight and say, "There's more than is dreamed of in your philosophy." Certainly these facts are interesting and deserve to be considered. But they are entitled only to a share of attention, and not a large share. It is a low curiosity or lust of

115

structure, and it is separated by celestial diameters from the love of spiritual truths. It is wholly a false view to couple these things in any manner with the religious nature and sentiment, and a most dangerous superstition to raise them to the lofty place of motives and sanctions. This is to prefer halos and rainbows to the sun and moon. These adepts have mistaken flatulency for inspiration. Were this drivel which they report as the voice of spirits really such, we must find out a more decisive suicide. The whole world is an omen and a sign. Why look so wistfully in a corner. Man is the image of God. Why run after a ghost or a dream?

This last reference to looking wistfully into corners suggests once again the image of the prison in which we confine our experience. In the conduct of life, escape from these corners in which we huddle is the first of the "great points" upon which human culture must be founded.

7

THE ESCAPE FROM
ALL FALSE TIES

Seldom published except in the *Works of Emerson* (1903), are Emerson's essays entitled "The Conduct of Life," which were delivered in lecture form beginning in 1851 and published finally in 1860. The complete series, including "Worship" and "Considerations By The Way," has recently been reprinted in the Library of America collection of Emerson's works (1983), making these important essays available once again to the reading public. In the series Emerson addressed the fundamental question "How shall I live?" He divided his subjects according to the limits we face and the problems we encounter. The essays, including the two mentioned above, cover "Fate," "Power," "Wealth," "Culture," "Behavior," "Beauty," and "Illusions." Once completed, this series rounds out the full circle promised in *Nature*.

There is a paragraph which concludes "Considerations by the Way" which lays out the essential points of the conduct of life:

> The secret of culture is to learn that a few great points steadily reappear, alike in the poverty of the obscurest farm and in the miscellany of metropolitan life, and that these few are alone to be regarded;—the escape from all

false ties; courage to be what we are; and love of what is simple and beautiful; independence and cheerful relation, these are the essentials,—these, and the wish to serve,—to add somewhat to the well-being of men.

"Illusions" is a tribute to the power of deception, to its victory over all our efforts to see clearly, and a reminder of the necessity to see beyond the tricks and games of life. In one of his notebooks, entitled "Orientalist," Emerson sets the stage for a discussion of illusion and its relation to the escape from false ties.

In the history of intellect no more important fact than the Hindoo theology, teaching that the beatitudes or Supreme Good is to be obtained through science; namely, by perception of the real and unreal, setting aside matter, and qualities and affections, or emotions and persons and actions as *Maias* or illusions, and thus arriving at the contemplation of the One Eternal Life and Cause and a perpetual approach and assimilation to Him; thus escaping new births and transmigration.

The highest object of their religion was to restore that bond by which their own self (*atman*) was linked to the Eternal Self (*paramatman*); to recover that unity which had been clouded and obscured by the magical illusions of reality, by the so-called Maia of Creation.

There is no clearer statement in all of Emerson's work both of his later debt to Eastern teachings and of his assertion that illusion is the great barrier to freedom. The Hindu teaching from the Vedas on the subject of Maia, or illusion, says again and again that the tyranny of the senses deceives us at every turn, that we are owned by the illusions that play in the mind and veil the truth in every moment that we give our attention to them.

118

The release from illusion allows for the establishment of what Emerson referred to as the link between the smaller self (*atman*) and the eternal self (*paramatman*), which he equates with the Over-Soul. Since illusion is the greatest of the false ties and includes the whole psychology of being, escape from this bondage is the only way to establish a link between a self paralyzed by illusion and a larger self which by definition is free of it.

The psychological illusions that occupy the mind and dictate our lives are so common and pervasive that we are scarcely aware of them in common hours. We may categorize them as rationalizations, justifications, day-dreams, and random inner conversations, almost all aimed at explaining to ourselves what the world is, what other people think of us, what we think of others, and how we are going to survive the seeming chaos of another day. Also, we all find ourselves in states of bondage called habit, false opinions, inherited circumstance, pointless labor, externally imposed expectations, and simple ignorance. These are the illusions of circumstance and appear to be the more substantial.

The first step in dispelling these illusions is to see them, but as Emerson affirms, nothing is more comforting than an illusion. We do not appreciate those who point out illusory thought or activity, so identified we are with our comforting games and masquerades. Emerson suggests that overcoming these "pillows," as he calls them, is a matter of strictness, faith and severity of purpose:

> In this kingdom of illusions we grope eagerly for stays and foundations. There is none but a strict and faithful dealing at home and a severe barring out of all duplicity or illusion there. Whatever games are played with us, we must play no games with ourselves, but deal in our privacy with the last honesty and truth. I look upon the simple and childish virtues of veracity and honesty as the root of all that is sublime in character. Speak as you think, be what

you are, pay your debts of all kinds. I prefer to be owned as sound and solvent, and my word as good as my bond, and to be what cannot be skipped, or dissipated, or undermined, to all the *eclat* in the universe. This reality is the foundation of friendship, religion, poetry and art.

("Illusions")

Honesty with ourselves is the challenge, and the attending painful process of truth-telling. The account is told of the students of Pythagoras, who, at the end of each day, were to review three times in mind every word, thought, and action that had transpired during the day, this for the purpose of releasing the mind from illusion. It took three accountings just to erase the ordinary illusions from the narrative, and even then the tale must have been full of imagined drama.

Much of the illusion that occupies the mind is defense of opinion. When Emerson gave his Divinity School Address in 1838, a storm of criticism and debate followed over the content and motivation behind the speech. Emerson's friends defended him and pleaded with him not to publish the transcript. He went ahead with limited publication because the students requested it, but at the same time he refused to debate in the public forum the issues raised by the content. For him all debate was illusion. The truth as he saw it lay behind the language in the address; nothing more could be said, at least until there was further inspiration on the same topic for another address or essay.

He did, however, write a poem, entitled "Uriel" in response to the controversy. In the poem the young god Uriel speaks the truth about the laws that govern the universe and thereby incurs the wrath of the older gods, shaming him to silence. But the force of truth is too great, even in the presence of gods. The poem concludes:

> But now and then, truth-speaking things
> Shamed the angels' veiling wings;

And, shrilling from the solar course,
Or from fruit of chemic force,
Procession of a soul in matter,
Or the speeding change of water,
Or out of the good of evil born,
Came Uriel's voice of cherub scorn,
And a blush tinged the upper sky,
And the gods shook, they knew not why.

The "procession of a soul in matter" is Emerson's metaphor for the self-recovering destiny of every life lived consciously and without illusion within the laws of nature (the solar course, chemic force, and the speeding change of water). It is this procession that is the point and not the debate involving particulars. Emerson lived by this principle throughout his life, and even the likes of Henry James could not draw him into critical discussions of past work. What was said was gone, and what was yet to come had simply to be awaited.

On the more personal and emotional plane, the task of breaking the bondage of illusion was much more difficult, particularly when it involved loss through death. The two most devastating losses for Emerson were his first wife, Ellen (in 1831), and his first son and namesake, Waldo (in 1842). In both cases he visited their graves often, and in both cases took the bold and horrifying step of looking into the coffin at the remains well after burial had taken place. In Ellen's case, he made a journal entry on March 29, 1832, " I visited Ellen's tomb & opened the coffin" (*JMN*, IV, p.7). As Gay Allen points out there is no reason to assume that this curt entry is not a factual statement (*Waldo Emerson*, p. 182). The burial had taken place in the family mausoleum in Roxbury, so the task of opening the coffin would not have involved digging into the earth. Nonetheless, the act must be seen as morbid in the extreme unless what lay behind it was Emerson's desire to rid himself of haunting illusions. The corpse is a natural thing and decays according to inviolate laws.

In 1857, fifteen years after little Waldo's death, on the occasion of the dedication of the new Sleepy Hollow Cemetery in Concord, Emerson moved the remains of his mother and his son to the new Emerson family plot. Again, he notes, "I ventured to look into the coffin."

These macabre notes display a "severe" dedication to the truth and affirm the conviction that the realm of illusion covers all material existence. Haunted by memory, Emerson cleansed the mind with the natural processes of decay. It was more than a matter of objectivity or scientific curiosity. It is not difficult, after all, to imagine the decay of a human body after death. Without embalming or the protection of a modern concrete-encased coffin, decay would be rapid. For Emerson, the illusions which haunted his mind were difficult to erase. Here, perhaps, was a way. We are reminded again of his youthful cry to the universe, ". . . thou art not my mother; Return to chaos if thou wilt, I shall still exist." If Emerson was to live according to such divine laws, he had to take drastic steps.

EMERSON'S FALSE TIES

Besides the false ties of illusion in the mind, there are those connected to the circumstances of the life, the choices made of profession, of a place to live, and of a style of existence. The escape from these false ties are also a gate to freedom. In Emerson's life there are the facts that his father, William Emerson, died when Waldo was eight, or nearly so, leaving his family destitute. He was brought up by his mother, with help from his redoubtable Aunt Mary. There were four brothers, of whom William was the oldest by two years. Waldo went to the Boston Latin School and then off to Harvard at the age of fourteen. During the summers and vacations of his years at college he worked as a tutor in his uncle's school. After college, at eighteen, he began teaching full-time until, two years later, he returned to Harvard to enter the School of Divinity. Beginning at age sixteen, he began keeping his journals and throughout this period also wrote many letters which have survived. These are the unadorned facts of his early life.

If we choose to color these facts with a particular system of thought, we can arrive at interpretations of actions, motives for statements, and reasons for belief. Psychological systems, which serve as illusions of meaning, have been used to speculate much about the loss of Emerson's father and his being thrust at such a tender age into the adult world. His search for a father, the absence of a suitable adult male, and the subsequent "discovery" of a spiritual stance outside normal family bonds have been offered as the basis of his transcendentalism. This form of reductive analysis focuses more on the system and deflects attention from the subject. In this form of critical opinion-making, therefore, the object (Emerson) becomes subservient to the system being applied because he becomes the object of analysis and his work becomes subservient to that end. It is another form of illusion.

This form of analysis is normative in the world of ideas. What can be destructive in it is the bondage to such opinion, the emotional and intellectual attachment to the game. Why else would we take offense when an idea we hold is challenged? Why would we defend a position long after it has been proven false by the presence of contradictory evidence? The passionate search for the facts and the passionate defense of opinions arising from them are two different ways of being in the world, the latter being a form of bondage. Emerson's genius is that he understood this level of confinement and devoted his life to breaking free of it.

Again and again we are confined by false notions in the form of opinion and attachment to ideas which have no value to the aim of self-recovery. We are imprisoned by the claim we make on an idea or an opinion. We often identify ourselves totally with the opinions we hold. In fact, for many people, we *are* the opinions we hold. We actually take our identity from them, and for many it is the basis of existence. Actually, what a man *does* is his belief and his reputation.

One of life's most challenging tasks is to separate the facts and events from ideas and opinions about them. Our great desire for clarity arises primarily from this need to separate the gold of fact from the dross of opinion, or, simply, to separate reality from illusion. In spiritual terms, reality is the realm of the divine, where truth resides. Nature is the realm where the laws are revealed to the waiting mind. It is where Emerson chose to live and to have his being. He described the nature of reality and illusion in a classical trope:

> Every god is there sitting in his sphere. The young mortal enters the hall of the firmament; there is he alone with them alone, they pouring on him benedictions and gifts, and beckoning him up to their thrones. On the instant, and incessantly, fall snow-storms of illusions. He fancies himself in a vast crowd which sways this way and that and whose movement and doings he must obey: he fancies himself poor, orphaned, insignificant. The mad crowd drives hither and thither, now furiously commanding this thing to be done, now that. What is he that should resist their will, and think or act for himself? Every moment, new changes, and new showers of deceptions to baffle and distract him. And when, by and by, for an instant, the air clears and the cloud lifts a little, there are the gods still sitting around him on their thrones,—they alone and him alone. ("Illusions")

Rejections, insults, praise, flatteries of all kinds, rewards, honors, blame, criticism, all are illusions in the sphere where this *god* resides. When the world rushes in with its demands, "furiously commanding" as it seems to do all the time, there is only one sane response: to reject the command in favor of clarity. Experience alone teaches, and the task is to watch and learn. Events seem heartbreakingly real, but their true value is in the observation of them. Emerson clarifies the point:

> The intellectual life may be kept clean and healthful, if man will live the life of nature, and not import into his mind difficulties which are none of his. No man need be perplexed in his speculations. Let him do and say what strictly belongs to him, and, though very ignorant of books, his nature shall not yield him any intellectual obstructions and doubts. Our young people are diseased with the theological problems of original sin, origin of evil, predestination, and the like. These never presented a practical difficulty to any man.
>
> ("Spiritual Laws")

Our philosophical and theological speculations are often passionately debated, as if our lives depended on them. What creates the passion is being wedded to these speculations and opinions, so that personal worth and identity is bound up with them. Verse 57, Book 2 of the *Gita* reads: "Who everywhere is free from all ties, who neither rejoices or sorrows if fortune is good or is ill, his is a serene wisdom." We are reminded that it was the *Gita* that Emerson took with him to the shore during the summer to renew and restore balance in his life.

EMERSON'S FIRST ESCAPE

Emerson's life is the example for the escape from false ties and the assumption of an authentic life. Emerson was born into a world of formal religion. In fact, he literally inherited his father's mantle, so early thrown off by the elder Emerson's untimely death. Waldo felt pressures from several sources to pick it up. Although he was left free from overt pressure by his family in order to discover his own destiny, the pull by heritage and taste to the role of minister was still very strong.

125

His preparation for the role of minister was undertaken from the outset with hesitation and ambiguity. From early in 1823, when Emerson was twenty, until his acceptance of the position of Junior Minister of the Second Church of Boston in 1829, Emerson struggled with the conflict between his personal religious views and the positions of the Church he was to serve. In this struggle of conscience versus traditional dogma, much has been made of an incident when his brother William, also in preparation for the ministry during this same period, paid a visit to the venerable Goethe in Weimar, Germany, in 1824.

William had been studying theology at the university in Gottingen for two years and had been struggling with the liberal intellectualism of the German thinkers in the light of his own more conservative background. The attacks of reason on the mythus of Christianity left him little room, so he thought, to maneuver when he envisioned his return to New England to preach. The conflicts had become the reality of his struggle rather than the ground of his exploration, and as a result, when he made a pilgrimage to Weimar to see the great Goethe, it is evident that he was fully identified with this conflict and would ask the wise man for advice.

In the fall of 1824 William appeared at Goethe's door, there to be received by the old man (then seventy-five) for a brief thirty-minute audience. They talked initially of America, the New England church and, finally arrived at William's own intellectual struggles. In William's own account of the interview, Goethe gave him the following advice:

He said he thought we had nothing to do with the different systems of philosophy, but that the highest aim of life should be for each one to accommodate himself as perfectly as possible to the station in which he was placed.

It appears from William's subsequent comments and actions that he took this advice to mean that he should compromise his standards, ignore his conscience, and conform himself to the confines of Unitarianism—this from the man whose life and work had been devoted to the struggle for inner authenticity. For a man identified with his intellectual struggles, William's reaction was a logical interpretation of the advice he was given. What is clear, however, is that the wisdom of the great man may have been offering a way out of his struggle by the simple and direct suggestion to direct his intellect and devotion to whatever was placed in front of him and to ignore the inner struggle. To "accommodate himself as perfectly as possible" is to say that our primary business and our path to authenticity lies in meeting the need in front of us in the moment that it arises. A minister is not primarily a theologian conforming theories to actualities, but rather is a man of the spirit helping his congregants to see their experience in the face of spiritual realities and aspirations.

William's subsequent decisions to renounce his faith and to become a lawyer in New York might be seen as an authentic escape from false ties were it not for the subsequent evidence of his life. He never made much of his chosen profession and even seemed to prefer giving lectures on literary subjects to parlor audiences to carrying out the duties of a lower court judge. Goethe may have been giving him the best advice of his life, but the intellectual conflict within which he was thoroughly confined did not permit him to hear accurately.

In Waldo's case, however, if the pressures were similar, the results were different. In the two years between 1827 and 1829 Emerson filled various pulpits throughout New England as a "supply" preacher. He found immediate success as a speaker, enjoying the traveling and the opportunity to meet the leading citizens of the various communities he visited. The experience of writing and delivering sermons on these occasions involved some careful side-stepping around troublesome issues while still meeting the needs of his hearers. We do not see in this period any undue agony over dogma.

What did begin to become clear, however, was that his true calling was not as a minister in the limited sense of pastoral visits and church duties. As his brother Charles said in a letter to William Emerson,

> He visits his people without any other guide or introduction, than his own knowledge of the street wherein they live. And thus he has sometimes made long calls, kindly & affectionate on families who had no other claim to his attention, than that of bearing the same name with his parishioners. (*Letters*, I, 270n)

The image of the kindly, affectionate, forgetful preacher dutifully sitting in a strange parlor is not the Emerson we meet in his work. Had he remained a minister, his vision would have been forever constricted by Unitarianism, and he would have joined the narrower ranks of thinkers such as Cotton Mather and William Channing in the history of American letters. In effect, the Church for Emerson was a false tie not because of what *it* was, but rather because of what *he* was. The gift he possessed had to find a more expansive and radical setting.

In that sense the advice given William by Goethe might have been too limiting. In saying that our task is to accommodate ourselves to the station in which we are placed, Goethe may have misled his young guest. Of course, the message may have been directed in the moment to the young man Goethe saw before him. Also, however, Goethe may have meant that our task was to merge our talents and constitution to the circumstances of our existence in order to become whole. Goethe's works contain that range of articulation. The word "station" used in William's account suggests profession rather than circumstances, which may have led him to the sense of being confined to a way of life. What Waldo did in the years between 1827 and 1832, when he resigned from the Second Church, was to accommodate his circumstances to the vision he had of his own gifts, not in the sense of ambition but in the sense of making real his inner knowledge of himself. His "station" was that of teacher to an entire culture. The pulpit of the Second Church was simply too small.

This vision was of a very high order, and it is worth experiencing some of its power. On April 17, 1827, during his trip to the South to recover his health, Emerson wrote:

> There is a pleasure in the thought that the particular tone of my mind at this moment may be new in the Universe; that the emotions of this hour may be peculiar & unexampled in the whole eternity of moral being. I lead a new life. I occupy new ground in the world of spirits, untenanted before. I commence a career of thought & action which is expanding before me into a distant & dazzling infinity. Strange thoughts start up like angels in my way & beckon me onward. I doubt not I tread on the highway that leads to the Divinity. (*JMN*, III, p. 79)

His financial condition, feelings of obligation, and strong ancestral heritage may have led him initially to conclude that the proper name of this highway to Divinity was Minister, but, once named, immediate regrets and promptings came from within to cast it off for something larger, something with fewer limits to spiritual expression. It would take him only two years to realize that he had made a mistake. Combined with this realization, of course, was the experience of losing his young wife Ellen, who succumbed to tuberculosis on February 8, 1831, after only sixteen months of marriage. The next year was a period of grieving and deep reflection for the young widower. During this period he took issue with his church on the practice of communion, asserting that Jesus had never intended to ritualize the Last Supper. He asked the Second Church to make communion less a matter of ritual and more a spontaneous "commemoration" of the life of faith. The church balked. He increased the pressure. A short reprise was arranged in the summer of 1832 while Emerson retired to the White Mountains of New Hampshire to reflect.

On July 14, he wrote,

> I would think—I would feel. I would be the vehicle of that divine principle that lurks within & of which life has afforded only glimpses enough to assure me of its being.

The next day he recorded the state of his mind as a reflection of nature:

> A few low mountains, a great many clouds always covering the great peaks, a circle of woods to the horizon.... The hour of decision....

In the same entry he debated with himself the usefulness of communion and the hope that his personal objections were not based on arrogance or willfulness. "The most desperate scoundrels have been the over refiners," he said of his own introspections. He knew full well the dangers of this intellectual game he might be playing.

On September 9, 1832, Emerson read his sermon on the Last Supper to his congregation, ending it with a brief statement of his resignation. In October, he made the following entry in his journal, writing his thoughts in a free-form style, reflecting the emotional release of his escape from the ministry:

> I will not live out of me
> I will not see with others eyes
> My good is good, my evil ill
> I would be free—I cannot be
> While I take things as others please to rate them
> I dare attempt to lay out my own road
> That which myself delights in shall be Good
> That which I do not want,—indifferent,

That which I hate is Bad. That's flat
Henceforth, please God, forever I forgo
The yoke of men's opinions. I will be
Lighthearted as a bird & live with God.

Free now to experience the natural sources of growth, he was to write several days later, "All true greatness must come from internal growth." And before the end of the year he had set sail for Europe, making his escape complete. The record of his thought shows a remarkable clarity in his reflections and a level of detachment uncommon in one so young. The relation of Ellen's death to his decision to leave the Church may have its source in the role that grief plays in our thinking. Grief has the power to create a space within which accurate reflection takes place. The space vacated in our hearts and minds by the loss of a loved one is of sufficient purity to be filled by an important and new perception of reality. In that sense our loss is our gain.

THE BONDAGE OF IDEAS

We saw in Emerson's struggle, reflected most clearly in his journals, how an idea in the form of opinion can hold us in a prison of our own making. We are all "over refiners" when it comes to the ideas that dominate our thinking and thus control our lives. We have ideas about what constitutes duty, responsibility, freedom, obligation, good and evil, justice, repentance, to name only a few of the major realms in which ideas play and engage us as thinking human beings. More than this general pattern we also have ideas about our own identity, built up over the years and reinforced by those who have a stake in our ignorance. We have ideas about our abilities and disabilities, about capacities and incapacities. One moment we are happy and the next miserable, mostly under the influence of these illusions.

In "Intellect" Emerson explored this last frontier of bondage. He said about it, "We have little control over our thoughts. We are the prisoners of ideas." That is not an attractive prospect. Just as we suppose that we might escape from the various false ties of our habitual lives, fleeing the destructive influences that keep us prisoner, we discover that we cannot escape our own thoughts, those shifting, floating, fragmentary words and pictures that most of the time run the show. Our love of Hamlet comes from his powerful clarity about the domination of thought, the twisting of reality in the distorted twilight.

The intellect is an organ of mind capable of sublime reflection and penetrating, detached understanding. It is the receptacle of Reason in the human instrument. Emerson is as clear as anyone about the relation of mind, thought, intellect, idea, understanding, knowledge, and about their relation to truth. Words and images that commonly blend together into a tangle of mental activity in our ordinary perception of thought were quite distinct in Emerson's own mind.

Why is it that, when we are too tired to think, suddenly we understand something that evaded our understanding in so-called "working" hours? Why is it that knowledge arises to solve a particular problem when we are not consciously or deliberately thinking about it? Why do ideas stay in the mind, moving and shifting about endlessly, holding our attention until we think we might go mad?

Emerson's answers to these questions emerged gradually from years of reflection on the nature of the intellect. His conviction was that the human mind was the link to divine knowledge and understanding. As such, it had to be divine in its own form and function. For him, there were no questions that could be posed by the human mind that would not eventually yield answers. The growth of the inner being had its focus in the development of the intellect. The mind had to be brought into harmony with the Universal Mind, which in its structure could be made one with the human mind.

The escape from false ties in the mind comes from the release of the intellect from its connection to the lower forms of mental activity.

The intellect goes out of the individual, floats over its own personality, and regards it as a fact, and not as *I* and *mine*. He who is immersed in what concerns person or place cannot see the problem of existence. This the intellect always ponders. Nature shows all things formed and bound. The intellect pierces the form, overleaps the wall, detects intrinsic likeness between remote things and reduces all things to a few principles. ("Intellect")

This floating intellect sees principle and loves it, cleaves to it as its own and will not let go unless driven away by madness. The intellect is the true metaphysical instrument, probing the limits of being even as the individual moves about the world conducting his or her business. True ideas are born in the intellect. They are the shapes of principles, given form by experience and expressed by circumstances.

Plato showed human beings the capacity to reflect consciously about abstract principles from within, calling upon a reference point not initially established on the authority of an external historical source. God for Plato was the Good, as perceived, grasped and understood in the fire of the intellect and then expressed in the life acted out as Justice.

At some stage of life, all thinking beings have to meet the crisis of authority. If the final, personal source of law in life is to be the conscience, then we must know the nature of that entity. For Emerson, the conscience was "essentially absolute, [but] historically limitary" ("The Conservative"). The Over-soul was the ultimate authority for the human being, whose intellect had the capacity to receive its intimations as principles by which to live. Therefore, an idea, in order to be true, must be formed out of principle in the intellect, and the test of its veracity is Platonic: simple, permanent, uniform and self-existent.

133

When we live from the ideas formed in the intellect, we are finally free of all false ties. The next step is to find the courage to live in that freedom.

8

THE COURAGE TO
BE WHAT WE ARE

In "Self-Reliance" Emerson said, "There is a class of persons to whom by all spiritual affinity I am bought and sold; for them I will go to prison if need be." In esoteric terms, "spiritual affinity" does constitute a class. It is made up of those who, while not necessarily following a particular religion or creed, yet regard spiritual questions and concerns as a vital force in life. They are Thoreau's "one in a hundred million," in terms of aspiration if not enlightenment. Emerson viewed this class as a natural aristocracy.

Throughout Emerson's work there is displayed an allegiance to this class and a general disdain for the self-satisfied, the cynical, the violent and the careless. The rebellious he watched cautiously for signs of true direction. The arrogant he avoided at all cost. The lost and ignorant were regarded with compassion and tenderness. But if someone came to him and said, "I, too, want to know how to find the spiritual truth by which I can live my life," Emerson put aside his own work to accommodate that desire.

What Emerson called the formation of the soul is the erect position, the stance in which we possess self-poise. The initial impulse comes by grace, but the journey once begun is sustained by concentration and by discipline. The active pursuit of such a journey in life allows for action in accordance with principles. Emerson called it dignity, nobility, self-possession. It is in this sense that Emerson viewed the seeker as an aristocrat, even a god. His Orphic voice in *Nature*, said:

> Man is the dwarf of himself. Once he was permeated and dissolved by spirit. He filled nature with his overflowing currents. Out from him sprang the sun and moon; from man the sun, from woman, the moon. The laws of his mind, the periods of his actions externized themselves into day and night, into the year and the seasons.

And so, he said again and again, it may be so again, being what we are. It is not a matter of magic or playing at God. The human condition at every level and stage is the same as consciousness of it. What we see is what we get, through a glass darkly or tinted in rose, or in the clarity of detached observation. The truth arrives through "lowly listening" and what we might call a reflective obedience freed from false ties.

COMPLETENESS

The goal is integration, bringing the impulses and elements of our nature into harmony. In great art the heart is opened to a larger world than we are able to perceive when we are self-centered. In the harmonious activity of the intellect we are capable of great understanding, particularly when we have the insight to know how we are ruled by false ideas and attitudes. In the devotions of religion we have the capacity for transformation when we see beyond the narrow, parochial concerns of habitual forms, but only when we surrender desire or expectation.

Regardless of the means, then, unity is the desired end, and unity comes only from harmonizing the elements of our being. Emerson called this harmony "completeness," and in his late essay "Greatness" he said that this ultimate aim of the spiritual

136

life came later, "perhaps adjourned for ages." In ordinary existence our fragmented lives stagger from one impulse or
demand to another, and we wonder if we might ever know the
harmony of the whole. In the meantime, however, we might
aspire, he said, to greatness, that perfection of our earthly
being which is inherent in each person at birth. Indeed if we
are ever to know "what we are," we have to move beyond the
fragmented self to a larger view and to accept, if only in theory
at first, the concept of unity proposed by Emerson and his
spirit-seeking company.

Central to this harmonious vision is Emerson's view that the
laws of the mind must be integrated into their proper hierarchy. Although Emerson never wrote an essay specifically
devoted to the laws of the mind, his biographer and editorial
assistant in later years, James Elliot Cabot, assembled journal
entries and essay sections on the subject in order to present a
coherent picture:

> These laws are ideas of Reason; they astonish the Under-
> standing, and seem to it as gleams of a world in which we
> do not live. Our compound nature differences us from
> God, but our reason is not to be distinguished from the
> Divine Essence. To call it ours seems an impertinence, so
> absolute and unconfined is it. The best we can say of God
> we mean of the mind as it is known to us. Time and space
> are below its sphere; it considers things according to
> more intimate properties; it beholds their essence,
> wherein is seen what they can produce. It is in all men,
> even the worst, and constitutes them men. In bad men it
> is dormant, in the good efficient; but it is perfect and
> identical in all, underneath the peculiarities, the vices,
> and the errors of the individual. Compared with the self-
> existence of the laws of truth and right, of which he is
> conscious, his personality is a parasitic, deciduous atom.
>
> The Understanding is the executive faculty, the hand of
> the mind. It mediates between the soul and inert matter. It

works in time and space, and therefore successively. The ideas of Reason assume a new appearance as they descend into the Understanding; they walk in masquerade. Reason, seeing in objects their remote effects, affirms the effect as the permanent character. The Understanding, listening to Reason on one side, which saith It is, and to the senses on their side, which say It is not, takes middle ground, and declares, It will be.

Heaven is the projection of the ideas of Reason on the plane of the Understanding. The Understanding accepts the oracle, but, with its short sight not apprehending the truth, declares that in futurity it is so, and adds all manner of fables of its own. What a benefit if a rule could be given whereby the mind, dreaming amidst the gross fogs of matter, could at any moment *east* itself and find the sun! But the common life is an endless succession of phantasms, and long after we have dreamed ourselves recovered and sound, light breaks in upon us, and we have yet had no sane hour. Another morn rises on mid-noon.

(*A Memoir of Ralph Waldo Emerson*, II, p. 246)

"The best we can say of God is the mind as it is known to us" is the foundation of what Emerson perceived to be the true nature of the human being. Admitting divinity to the mind, equating and integrating whatever that means to the concept of Man Thinking that Emerson introduced in "The American Scholar" opens our thought to the presence of full power and divine presence. It is an immensely courageous act, and unless it is done in utter humility, the proper hierarchy can never be established. It is as much an act of faith as a perception of the intellect, and it only appears to be a contradiction of human understanding.

Emerson found the way to overcome the conflict between belief, his God-in-the-mind, on the one hand and intellectual freedom and individuality, on the other. He was presented a received tradition which would not stand up to intellectual scrutiny of the first order. He then had to do one of two things—or so it seemed: either deny his own intellectual integrity in favor of a system of belief, or jettison his beliefs in favor of his intellectual integrity and trust that belief would rise to meet that freedom.

He chose the latter path, resigning from the Unitarian Church and striking out into the intellectual and spiritual wilderness on his own. What he discovered there was a way to proceed in absolute integrity. The mind, he found, was the world in which he would discover possibilities. Belief in the mind and belief in God became the same. God was by definition infinite and eternal, while the mind, by the normal standards, had to be limited and mortal.

To find the way in which mind could be known as infinite and eternal became the aim of his intellectual life. Emerson did not so much look for specific answers to perennial questions as he looked for lines of energy along which he might find enough truth to take his next step. To that extent, he recognized the limits of human perception. We do not find the truth, he said again and again, so absolute a thing is it. What we find instead is the means to render ignorance transparent, through which the truth may one day be glimpsed.

He found in Plato the way through the barriers of ignorance. Plato bridged the unity of the East and the diversity of the West. The essay on Plato plots the points on the map of Emerson's intellectual voyage. Others had the vision; Plato showed the way for the intellect. The key was to see that the human mind was made up of a hierarchy. In the ruling position was the Over-Soul or universal mind shared by all, including God. It was called Reason by Emerson. The cursive mind, the executive faculty, also called Understanding, was finite. It was formed by the stuff of individuality and was different from one person to the next. The promptings of the higher mind, Reason, were instinctive and intuitive. This mind did not speak, and it had no words. It functioned in us in great stillness, but could be thought of as a light. It was apprehended in moments of pure reflection. Its promptings, then, were qualitative, recognized by the heart and articulated by the imagination. To live in the spirit meant to follow the light of Reason.

To live a spiritual life meant to develop this universal mind as the ruling principle of the individual life. Obedience to its promptings was the key to happiness, fulfillment, and eternal life. Emerson saw the promise of a future heaven as the deception of those who sought to preserve the cursive mind forever. The poem "Brahma" is an image of this hierarchy of mind:

> If the red slayer think he slays,
> Or if the slain think he is slain,
> They know not well the subtle ways
> I keep, and pass, and turn again.
>
> Far or forgot to me is near;
> Shadow and sunlight are the same;
> The vanished gods to me appear;
> And one to me are shame and fame.
>
> They reckon ill who leave me out;
> When me they fly, I am the wings;
> I am the doubter and the doubt,
> And I the hymn the Brahmin sings.
>
> The strong gods pine for my abode,
> And pine in vain the sacred Seven;
> But thou, meek lover of the good!
> Find me, and turn thy back on heaven.

When we are greedy to keep this limited consciousness alive for eternity, we cling to the idea of heaven for the lower consciousness. The universal mind, however, has no personality and no finite identity. Letting go of the personality is the way to eternal life. We have to die to live. As Jesus said, we have to lose our life in order to gain it.

THE REPRESENTATIVE MEN

The examples in history of more or less successful integration of higher orders of the mind are explored in *Representative Men*, the series of essays in which Emerson drew portraits of universal mind at work in nature. It was the shaping of his own higher thought, the making of the vision in human terms, and the framing of a whole individual from representatives. He chose partial men, those whose talents and lives might cohere into a single expression of integrated or Central Man.

The vision behind the collective images was Emerson himself, not in arrogance, but in idealism. His men are the philosopher, mystic, skeptic, poet, man of action, writer, all men of expression, each in a different sphere, articulating their unique sense of the truth with the world as a guide. They also all acted with courage.

In each case, these representative men guide us, through Emerson's pen, on the path of knowing what we are. Plato guides our spiritual intent to reveal the nature of the soul and the concept of the Good; Swedenborg gives us the purity and meaning of the symbolic universe; Montaigne gives us judgment, teaching us to watch carefully, with discrimination, before we believe or doubt; Shakespeare is the poet of human nature, teaching us to expand our vision of what human nature was capable of; in Napoleon, we marvel at the man who acts intuitively, using his time and circumstances to express human aspiration in the world; finally, there is Goethe, whose vision gives the soul expression.

It is Shakespeare, however, with whom we are most comfortable among these representatives. We know the plays, have been elevated and moved by the words, images and visions. So too was Emerson, and he took this genius as an example of what we are and might become, calling him "this man of men, he who gave to the science of mind a new and larger subject than had ever existed, and planted the standard of humanity some furlongs forward into Chaos." ("Shakespeare; Or The Poet").

141

That is, in fact, what our task is, this planting of the "standard of humanity some furlongs forward into chaos." A good definition of courage might be that quality which permits a bold step forward into the abyss. We see and hear that quality on the field of Agincourt when "We few, we happy few" advanced the cause of courage some few paces forward into the abyss of death.

THE COURAGE TO BE

The essay entitled "Courage" was written in 1859 in the aftermath of John Brown's attempt to arm the slaves at Harper's Ferry. In 1857 Brown had come to Concord and as Emerson said, "gave a good account of himself in the Town Hall... to a meeting of citizens." In the lecture on courage Emerson referred to Brown as "that new saint, than whom none purer or more brave was ever led by love of men into conflict and death,—the new saint awaiting his martyrdom, and who, if he shall suffer, will make the gallows glorious like the cross." This glorification of Brown's presence in a Virginia jail awaiting his death was left out of the essay when it was published ten years later in *Society And Solitude*, but it was clear that Emerson was deeply moved by Brown.

In 1861, at the outbreak of civil war, Emerson marveled at the power of the collective response to the outbreak of hostilities. He said, on that occasion, "I will never again speak lightly of a crowd" (Cabot, II, p. 218). He was conscious of the overwhelming energy that galvanized the citizens of the North and South to defend their sense of what was right. But for the essay on courage, he was thinking of John Brown because here was an action motivated by principle and was not a matter of politics or economics or personal ambition.

Oliver Wendell Holmes said that Emerson was qualified to speak on the subject because he had demonstrated great courage himself in speaking on slavery in public, particularly in commercial Boston, where there were powerful economic and emotional pro-slavery forces arrayed against the Abolitionists. On at least one occasion he was shouted off the podium by pro-slavery elements. In "The Fugitive Slave Law" Emerson had said, "The politics of Massachusetts are cowardly," referring to the acceptance in the Commonwealth of the law which made a crime of aiding and abetting the escape of a slave.

Emerson had said that real courage, "courage with eyes, courage with conduct, self-possession at the cannon's mouth, cheerfulness in lonely adherence to the right, is the endowment of elevated characters." Courage seizes the moment when, briefly, the eyes are opened to the truth of things, when the heart opens and the judgment affirms the course of action. "Cowardice...shuts the eyes of the mind and chills the heart" ("Courage"). What Emerson had perceived was the presence of the vital force of life itself in the expression of courage.

The courage to be what we are finds its expression in carrying a principle through the circumstances. Human beings are the means by which the divine law is expressed in matter. We are designed by nature to overcome entropy, not to express it. As we look at the world, we see the weakness, cowardice, corruption and decay. We may also be gifted enough to see the principles, laws, and actions which are needed to overcome them. In our cities today, taking the streets back from decay in all its forms is an act of courage. The impulse is quite beyond mere convenience. The anger we feel when ignorance, crime, and human degradation of all kinds pour from the darkest corners of the culture into the public thoroughfares comes from a natural outrage against the waste of human potential. Let vermin scurry out of a grating to grab a piece of food; that is their nature. But it is not a human being's. Dignity is a birthright, and it is denied everywhere.

The task in life is to carry this principle of dignity into the circumstances of existence. Dignity is not just good manners, although Emerson spoke well on that subject, too. Dignity has to do with human nature, with the truth emerging in action, in how we face the world. The loss of dignity cries out today among the aging, dying by degrees, wired to external life support in hospital wards; among the victims of AIDS, as they struggle with the limited hope of just dying with dignity; among the addicts left in the streets by the greed of pushers and dealers and the neglect of governments. It is not just a matter of money needed to correct these circumstances; it is a matter of dignity expressed by the courage of those who see and understand the nature of the struggle.

"In short, courage consists in equality to the problem before us" ("Courage"). Courage gives us the knowledge that the circumstances are never superior to our ability to overcome them. But most often, at least in the public sector, the need is for a collective act of courage. Society as a whole has to act. Even as the circumstances are oppressive and dangerous, so are they also illusory. If we realize that our business is with expressing natural law, then we can find the words and the detachment to use them well in the cause of elevation.

Put another way, the circumstances of life are surfaces, horizontal planes of matter and energy. The principles we carry about with us are all related to the vertical lines of energy that connect us to the sublime, rooted though we are in matter. Courage arises to meet the natural resistance of planes meeting at right angles to our experience. Every time we say "That's just not right!" and then act upon that stand, we help to describe a higher vision of human nature.

THE SUBSTANCE OF COURAGE

The earth revolves, the solar system revolves, the galaxy revolves, the universe revolves, all moving neither forward nor backward, but merely shifting according to laws of space and time. As Einstein taught us, space tells matter how to move, and matter tells space how to bend. Force on force. Consciousness is the subtle energy that maintains the difference between space and matter. In that difference, life, too, revolves and makes its claim in the universe.

There must be a connection between the attribute we call courage and the instruments that carry it into the circumstances of life. Emerson explores that connection in this way:

> It is plain that there is no separate essence called courage, no cup or cell in the brain, no vessel in the heart containing drops or atoms that make or give this virtue; but it is the right or healthy state of every man, when he is free to do that which is constitutional to him to do. It is directness,—the instant performing of that which he ought.
>
> ("Courage")

We do not have an easy time with "oughts," so loaded are they with thoughts of duty and responsibility imposed from without. The only circumstances when "ought" arises in front of us seem to occur when we are overcome by feelings of separation and fear. When what dominates our life is "I won't serve," then the magnets of duty are felt pulling on our minds and hearts. It is not difficult to ignore a duty that is not real, that is, one imposed artificially by the culture. It is much harder, however, to resist duty that we intuitively accept because it is right, but which we resist because fulfilling it will be inconvenient or dangerous.

But since we cannot know this essence at first hand, at least in the ordinary course of events, we must find the approximations of it in other ways. Courage, as Emerson points out, is the attribute that opens the gate or storms the walls of ignorance and fear.

> The best act of the marvelous genius of Greece was its first act; not in the statue or the Parthenon, but in the instinct which, at Thermopylae, held Asia at bay, kept Asia out of Europe, Asia with its antiquities and organic slavery,— from corrupting the hope and new morning of the West.

The statue, the architecture, were the later and inferior creation of the same genius. In view of this moment of history, we recognize a certain prophetic instinct, better than wisdom. ("Courage")

The Greek reliance on freedom and debate as opposed to the Persian dependence on slavery and coercion was born in the courageous defense of the Greek mainland (Attica) by a handful of foot soldiers. Later victories by the Athenian fleet, although impressive enough, were not the foundation for the development of the classical period which later served to advance Western culture. Emerson's point is that courage was the basis of the trust which created a new vision in human organization. It laid the foundations as well for Socrates, Plato, Aristotle, Greek tragedy and comedy and the brilliance of classical art. By contrast, we have nothing of comparable value from the Persian culture of the same period. Western culture was born in an act of courage. The kingdom of Darius I evaporated in defeat.

We see the same principle in operation in Shakespeare's treatment of the Battle of Agincourt in *Henry V*. The English army was outnumbered five to one by an over-confident French force. With little or no hope of surviving the battle, Henry and his brothers-in-arms gave up everything except the act of courage itself. There was no talk of cause or future gain in the result. The purity of the action resulted in a miracle, attributed by Henry later on to the will of God. The identity of God with the act of courage, with no other thought or motive intervening, created the circumstances of victory.

THE DOMINATION OF FEAR

In "Courage" Emerson connects the negative to the positive attribute by affirming, "He has not learned the lesson of life who does not every day surmount a fear." The first step in such a task is to recognize the fear to be surmounted and to be prepared for what is to come. As Emerson points out in "Success," the essay which follows "Courage" in *Society and Solitude*, Columbus was not fearful in his voyages because, as he said, "There is a mode of reckoning derived from astronomy, which is sure and safe to any one who understands it" ("Success"). It is also possible to understand the journey of the soul in matter to the same degree of assurance and safety, to the end that all fear of the journey melts away. Fear, then, is the signal we get when we know we are unprepared. The best response to that signal is not a false bravado that pushes through the fear, but rather a determination to erase the reason for the fear by being prepared. It is that preparation that Emerson means by defining courage as "equality to the problem before us."

WHAT WE ARE

Beyond the surfaces of life is where being what we are really matters. The Vedanta school of Hindu philosophy and religion uses a classic statement from the Vedas to define this identity. In Sanskrit the sentence is *tat twam asi*, or "That thou art," meaning that we are That Being which is the One and the Unity of all things. "I am nothing, I see all.... I am part or particle of God" was Emerson's statement of the principle. As That Being, the individual is not confined to a prison with cells of earthly identities.

The first connection we make with That Being is a simple knowledge of its existence. It becomes then a possibility, or an aspiration. We experience a notion of the transcendent in the heart as a feeling of great expansiveness. We identify that feeling as love, the Greek *agape*, as opposed to passion, *eros*. It is not an intellectual notion because we experience such knowledge as understanding, which is too far below the level of its existence.

When Emerson first published *Nature* with its account of Unity as transparent eyeball and its affirmation of identity with

God, reaction was swift and critical. A cartoon by Christopher Cranch appeared in the Boston papers showing Emerson as an eyeball, top-hatted, bare-footed and absurd. Cranch was actually sympathetic to these transcendental views and would later contribute a poem entitled "To the Aurora Borealis" to the first issue of the *Dial*. Emerson reacted with some surprise at the vehemence of the initial response, but otherwise paid little or no attention to the furor. It was, however, a clear indication of his separation from the mainstream and his new identity as a member of a new class.

Most critics interpret Emerson's work after *Nature* as the natural process of change tempered by experience, a falling away from principle in the light of the harsh lessons of life. Nothing in Emerson's life, however, including the death of loved ones, was more harsh than his early years of deprivation and personal illness. His later work was not a falling away from principle at all, but was rather a continuing refinement and clarification of his fundamental stand. Each essay was a sally of the mind intended to explain yet again what the original intuition had taught him. Each expression was a confirmation of what experience presented to his attention in the moment.

As a radical reformer, Emerson never thought that his idealism would ever take hold as an operative value system in American culture. He was too objective an observer of human nature and of the power of materialism to suppose that majorities would transform themselves as he had done. The courage he displayed was in his early recognition of the lonely path he was to take and in the determination he exhibited in staying the course.

9

SIMPLICITY, BEAUTY
AND INDEPENDENCE

Emerson's essay on Stone-henge, from *English Traits*, describes his visit in July, 1848 with Carlyle to the great Druid temple. Afterwards, on a rainy Sunday, confined to their lodgings, Carlyle challenged Emerson to elaborate a theory "of the right future" of America. Rising to the challenge, Emerson first declared that he would speak neither of "caucuses nor congress, neither presidents nor of cabinet-ministers, nor of such as would make America another Europe." Rather, he would expound in that moment another vision. He and Carlyle had, after all, just visited one of the world's truly sublime images of the cosmos, and the impression lingered of something profoundly beautiful and, at the same time, as Emerson described it "this simplest of all simple structures" ("Stonehenge"). There on Salisbury Plain in a series of four concentric stone rings was a unified perception of nature, humanity and God, expressed in sacred number, geometry, and architecture.

The two brief visits to Stonehenge that weekend had set the spiritual stage for fresh perceptions and radical thought. The ancient peoples who had assembled this temple knew what it meant to still the mind and to elevate the personal and collective consciousness from the banal to the sublime. The form of

Stonehenge drew the pilgrim into a coherent world view and evoked in Emerson and Carlyle as well the expanse of sacred traditions throughout Europe.

As originally conceived Stonehenge was a temple of the cosmos, an expression of divine principle made manifest by the great astronomical circle of stones indicating the geometric relationship between the earth, the heavens, and human life. The people who envisioned and built this temple gathered there to renew the ancient bonds of unity with the intelligence of the universe. In the presence of this sacred structure the mind unites with the manifest vision and sees differently, sees the unity present in all things, sees the eternal center.

As we noted earlier in the discussion of conversation and revelation, the minds of those who come together to speak of serious subjects soar to new heights in the common effort and more can be said and seen than in common hours. On that rainy Sunday in July of 1848, a year of revolution and chaos in Europe and fear of the same in England, three minds devoted to new thought—Emerson, Carlyle, and Arthur Helps, a writer and prominent political figure—sat at Helps' home in Bishops Waltham and discussed the future of America. It was a theme interesting to Carlyle in particular, who had drawn from Emerson on the train ride down to Salisbury the observation that England was a dying country and would live in future only in the accomplishments of its departed children. It was for the great Englishman an unwelcome thought, and he challenged Emerson that Sunday to say how and in what manner America would better the past glory of England. Emerson was asked specifically if there were any persons in America who had a true vision for the future of the country. He later wrote in his journal:

I thought only of the simplest and purest minds; I said, "Certainly yes;—but those who hold it are fanatics of a dream which I should hardly care to relate to your English ears, to which it might be only ridiculous,—and yet it is the

150

only truth." So I opened the dogma of no-government and non-resistance, and anticipated the objections and the fun, and procured a kind of hearing for it..., —and 'tis certain, as God liveth, the gun that does not need another gun, the law of love and justice, can alone effect a clean revolution.

The vision that Emerson dared speak of was central to the attitudes of many of his closest friends in America. With love and justice at the core, the self-reliant individual lived in a state of true independence, free from authority and yet obedient to natural law. Unlike the constituency of Plato's Republic where the philosopher-king ruled and the poets were banished, Emerson's American Republic was to be governed by the visionary sensibility.

Emerson's America would not find political expression until human beings were by that degree self-reliant. In fact, just two years before, Thoreau had gone to jail rather than pay a tax that would support the Mexican war. His simple act of civil disobedience and the essay that followed from it would later provide inspiration to Gandhi and Martin Luther King, who both applied non-resistance to social and political aims. As Emerson commented, the government could always count on men such as Webster to compromise on moral principle, but it could not count on the likes of Thoreau, as a representative of Central Man, to keep silent. If enough people could establish within themselves this self-governed way of being in the world, the life of the nation would open to a new era and a new order of life.

It was in the realm of social and political action that the idealism of the Transcendental movement failed to survive the American Civil War. As a personal, esoteric spiritual movement, it remains viable and is carried forward by anyone who discovers a sympathy of outlook and a means of expression for it. That Emerson would be drawn into broader speculations on that Sunday in Bishops Waltham was natural to him, particularly in the light of the Stonehenge visit. There, after all, was an expression of principle at the center of a viable human

151

culture, one with a long, albeit dim, history. Perhaps it could work again.

SIMPLICITY

To find the unity in diversity is the role of the seeker of laws. When we find the unity behind the complex array of nature, we find the inherent simplicity of nature and are home in it. We can never be at peace while we exist in a myriad of facts. ("Literary Ethics")

In its simplicity Stonehenge was an expression of the "unity behind the complex array of nature." Those who built it were seeking first the "inherent simplicity" of the source of unity. When Emerson spoke of the unity of law behind and beyond the appearances of things, he spoke at a time when such a view was susceptible of living proof in the daily experience of those who consciously sought such unity. Today, however, our experience is so inundated with particulars that we can barely make out a basic pattern of cause and effect. Subtle worlds of force and influence are lost on us. We can no longer carry out a simple task simply. Our sense of unity is likely to be expressed in simplistic language. We speak of the global village or the unifying effects of electronic communication, but such unity is an illusion and not relevant to our subject. In effect, we are shattered, nearly beyond repair, Emerson's "god in ruins."

What has not changed over the millennia is the human instrument itself, an image of the simplicity posited by Emerson. In his essay on Goethe there is a description of the sublime nature of the human organism:

It is the last lesson of modern science that the highest simplicity of structure is produced, not by few elements, but by the highest complexity. Man is the most composite of all creatures; the wheel-insect, *volvox globator,* is at the other extreme. ("Goethe; Or, The Writer")

We know more now about this composite nature of our own existence. We are not a single organism, but are a complex universe of organisms living in symbiosis. We extend beyond our body in dependency and influence and host myriads of complex societies of organisms which depend on our breathing, eating, and metabolism. Even the individual cells are composite creatures in the sense that they live out their lives in complex relation to their neighbors and environment.

The exercise of perceiving the simplicity of the single existence of the body as a whole amidst the complexity of existences to which it plays host is instructive. If we imagine, for example, that our lifetime of four score and ten years is an eternity in relation to the existence of a microbe that exists temporarily to keep our eyeball clean, we achieve a useful perspective. If we can speak of any degree of consciousness in the microbe, we can say that it knows little of its struggle to survive or of its constant activity in existence. It knows nothing of its host or of the beauty that is perceived through the organ on the surface of which it lives out its life. Its consciousness, therefore, is severely limited, nothing compared to that of its omniscient host, whose arcane thoughts construct theories of beauty, life, and death. Its knowledge, if we can speak at all of such a thing, is of its narrow function. It "knows" what to do and how to reproduce itself so that others in kind will assume the same task.

What could be more simple, however, than this whole, this universe we call a human being, especially when we see this creature express itself in eloquent speech, in dance, or in song. In such moments as these, the whole is harmonious, each part falling naturally into proper place in the hierarchy. When Emerson spoke of the "love of what is simple and beautiful" as one of the great points of culture, he meant all of this elegant perfection in human expression, the natural aristocracy of those "that have that simplicity and that air of repose which are the finest ornaments of greatness."

("Aristocracy")

BEAUTY

We ascribe beauty to that which is simple; which has no superfluous parts; which exactly answers its end; which stands related to all things; which is the mean of many extremes. ("Beauty")

In the *Conduct of Life* essays, "Beauty" follows the passage on the great points of culture in "Considerations by the Way." The organizing principle of the essay is this: "Beauty is the form under which the intellect prefers to study the world." As Emerson saw it, we are interested in relations, in the connection made by the intellect between and among the things of the world, and we have a natural preference for the pleasures of beauty as a means for such study. In addition to preference, however, beauty itself lies in connections. The beauty of the bird is not just in its flight or its feathers but also in its perceived relation to nature and to us. The emphasis, as always in Emerson, is on the laws that govern the existence of the bird. When we study the world, beauty is the gate to the place where the principles can be seen and explored. If we see the beauty, we see the form, and, hence, the principle cannot be far behind.

The beauty of a thing exists before the mind as a sign of direction. In that sense "beauty is the pilot of the young soul." Drawn by beauty, we know we are moving in the right direction. Without beauty as a guide, we cannot know whether or not the direction or influences we are following are positive and life-enhancing. The connection between beauty and simplicity helps us to distinguish between true beauty and that which is deceptively seductive to the senses. True beauty stills the mind and permits the intellect to "study the world." The merely seductive, on the other hand, stimulates the mind to distracting activity. It rouses desires in the realm of the banal, leaving us shattered and fragmented.

In Greek myths, Apollo and his lesser companion Pan competed annually in a musical contest in the sanctuary of Delphi, Apollo playing the stringed lyre while Pan played the flute. The music of the flute was seductive, entrancing to the senses, inducing forgetfulness in the hearer. The lyre of Apollo, on the other hand, was a harmonizing instrument, evocative of the consciousness of Zeus himself. In the contests, Apollo always won so that the lyre would always be associated with the sublime forces of the universe and the true expression of beauty. The flute was eventually banished from official contests on the grounds that it induced madness in the listener.

> When the act of reflection takes place in the mind, when we look at ourselves in the light of thought, we discover that our life is embosomed in beauty.

This familiar opening sentence from "Spiritual Laws" may now be seen in its full context. Beauty is the form perceived by the highest faculty of mind in the act of reflection. We naturally reside in the lap of a terrible beauty, terrible because it is devoid of sentimentality and utterly simple and just. It is also terrible because the emotion we describe as awe or wonder also has inherent within it an aspect of terror. If our ordinary experience is comfortable and banal, then revelatory experience is not, and the terror we experience at the edge of divinity in the country of the sublime is also terrifyingly beautiful.

INDEPENDENCE

It is in this very large view that the term "independence" can be applied to individual life in concert with beauty and simplicity of vision. If we are independent, we are free of the social restraint that dictates so much of our behavior. If we are fully independent, we owe nothing in thought or idea to anyone. We are not in debt to any thinker or purveyor of opinion or taste. The words we speak are not governed by anything but the truth of the moment of utterance. We are, in a word, self-reliant. Emerson's most important statement of self-reliance came when he asked a friend, "What have I to do with the sacredness of traditions, if I live wholly from within?" ("Self-Reliance")

It is only when the idea of independence is seen in this broad expanse of insight and natural law that it can rise above the limitations of personality. In the narrow world of ego, independence becomes separation, a world in which we shut ourselves off from others as well as from our own true nature. True independence is freedom in the highest sense; it is the same as spiritual liberation in Emerson's view.

For many seekers of spiritual truths and personal independence, the fatal error in the journey is to leave the world path and find solace and tranquility in the isolated way. What for the wise are moments of solitary reflection becomes for the escapist a permanent path of separation. Tens of thousands of unhappy people live in what Thoreau called "quiet desperation" in lonely rooms with drawn curtains because they have accepted the attraction of living in separation. The attraction is obvious enough. It is the pull of abdication, of running away instead of staying, of resigning instead of taking responsibility.

Our true business lies in connection and community. Emerson saw clearly that a state of independence or self-poise was essential to the health and vitality of any connection. Love is the emotion of connection, but self-love comes first and is the essential quality of independence. It is always an aspect of self-loathing that fires the passion of separation.

It is the argument of this study that the great essay of independence, "Self-Reliance," was meant for the individual seeker of spirit. That it has been read too much as the doctrine of American individualism and completely misread as the doctrine of selfishness speaks to a diminished view of human nature. It is, however, a testament to the dictum "Do what you must" and not an apology to an easy "Do what you want." Emerson saw that in an America only sixty years old when this essay was written there was a possibility that the growth and character of the nation could be characterized by sublime principles if only the individual could escape from the prisons of conformity and materialism to seek a truer freedom.

At this point the student might ask of Emerson, "But how do I become self-reliant? How do I overcome my ego and all the attractions of the world to find my true self?" Emerson answered:

> The relations of the soul to the divine spirit are so pure that it is profane to seek to interpose helps. It must be that when God speaketh he should communicate, not one thing, but all things; should fill the world with his voice; should scatter forth light, nature, time, souls, from the centre of the present thought; and new date and new create the whole. Whenever the mind is simple and receives a divine wisdom, old things pass away,—means, teachers, texts, temples fall; it lives now, and absorbs past and future into the present hour. All things are made sacred by relation to it,—one as much as another.
>
> ("Self-Reliance")

By holding us to the sacred principle, Emerson keeps the searching individual above the realm of personal solutions, which by definition are separate solutions. To seek specific advice about a specific situation is to reinforce the illusion of the separate personality. The great weakness of most

157

psychotherapy is just this tendency to begin with the notion of "what I want for myself in this situation" without any true sense on the part of therapist or patient of what the principles are. What is needed is a sublime therapy in which the individual under the guidance learns how to transform the banal and profane aspects of his or her life to gain release from bondage and enter the world of freedom.

There have been, in the twentieth century, indications of this kind of work, and no doubt there is evidence of real success. For example, Paul Diel, the late Austrian psychologist, left a record of successful treatment of individuals based on spiritual principles. Jung can also be credited with some success, although his own work remains too broadly based in myth to be applied to individual cases. Other Jungians have made real progress, however. What we learn from these efforts is that the whole direction of the life needs to be reversed, literally faced in the other direction, in order to find authentic release. A state of misery is usually the indication of a serious problem. In the opposite direction lies joy, which is a release from all sorts of miseries, both real and imagined.

CHEERFUL RELATION

Among Emerson's great points, independence is firmly connected to "cheerful relation," that state in which we exist happily in our circumstances. In his early life, Emerson knew from harsh experience the spiritual, emotional and intellectual cost of dependency. The decade between 1811, when his father died, and 1821, when he graduated from Harvard and began his independent career, was one of poverty and dependency. His mother, Ruth Haskins Emerson, had been left without financial resources for her family of seven and became dependent on a series of benefactors, including distant family and the officers of the Second Church, where her husband had been minister. The proud Emerson family, boasting a noble heredity in New England history, came very close to dissolution, both from want and from chronic illnesses.

The rich record in family letters and diaries leaves a trail of sadness and discouragement during this difficult period on everyone's part except Waldo's, who maintained a cheerfulness that lifted his family in moments of despair. The young Emerson was forced by circumstance to supervise and tutor his Uncle Ripley's schoolboys during his own Christmas vacation and at other times when a boy of only fifteen might want to be free to play. Nevertheless, Waldo, writing his brother, cheerfully recounted his first days as a teacher:

> Here I am surrounded by my 14 disciples, (Pythagoras &c called their scholars disciples I believe, & modesty forbids me to say how far superior I think myself to Pythagoras) every little while calling out, Silence! for school is just begun ie 1/2 after 8—but stop must hear them read—Hem — (*Letters*, I, 55–57)

It is easy enough to be cheerful when things are going well, but the effects of poverty and illness strike first at the emotional life and leave us sullen and moody at best. Emerson's detachment served him well in these trying conditions. There was no fault, after all, in his situation, no one to blame, least of all nature or even society. There was no assumption that the world owed him anything, as indeed it didn't. It would not have entered his mind that the Bill of Rights guaranteed him government support for "life, liberty and the pursuit of happiness." In 1818 there was no right to gainful employment or even the dignity of existence that many today deem to be a part of our rights as citizens. Far from being a political position, Emerson's attitude moved even beyond philosophy. It was spiritual, but it was also not bound to Puritanism or Calvinist thinking, which would have suggested a kind of passive suffering as a proper stance for the devout Christian.

Emerson's detachment has also been attributed to a cool personality, a fundamental lack of warmth in the boy and the man, perhaps stemming from his emotionally restrained upbringing and perhaps from an ebbing in his veins of physical vitality. Whatever the physiological facts, the boy Waldo was definitely not gregarious, seeking instead the pleasures of reading in the cellar room he occupied on Hancock Street, his window looking out at gravestones in the next lot. The fact of being withdrawn from human society is not, in and of itself, a sign of indifference to life or to other human beings. Waldo was from a young age a gifted poet, and the passion to express his visions in verse occupied his mind when others were at play or in conversation. His work and the biographies which followed his life make clear how deeply he loved and was loved in return by those who moved within his orbit.

In our own relations, the dual demands of independence and cheerful relation present a paradox of action, but in Emerson's view the two move together naturally. It is dependence that threatens our relationship to others. When we are not free to think and feel and act in the world, we close down the natural lines of feeling that would normally stay open and responsive to others.

Emerson's encouragements to us to be cheerful are a proof of his warmth of spirit. In "New England Reformers" he said, "That which befits us, embosomed in beauty and wonder as we are, is cheerfulness and courage, and the endeavor to realize our aspirations." Clear in this encouragement is the fundamental fact of how difficult it is to make real our aspirations without the aspect of good cheer in the endeavor. In "Considerations By The Way" this theme is explored in greater depth.

> Nothing will supply the want of sunshine to peaches, and to make knowledge valuable, you must have the cheerfulness of wisdom. Whenever you are sincerely pleased, you are nourished. The joy of the spirit indicates its strength. All healthy things are sweet-tempered. Genius works in

sport, and goodness smiles to the last; and for the reason that whoever sees the law which distributes things, does not despond, but is animated to great desires and endeavors. He who desponds betrays that he has not seen it.

Most of what we truly need is here: the relation between wisdom and good humor as proof. We have the clear indication of feeling as a measure of our depth of insight. Joy is the indication that we have penetrated to the foundation level of spirit. Nothing else measures the depth of perception as well. If a self-styled wise man argues in anger that his view of truth is the correct one, we can be sure that it is not. Cheerfulness and patience mark both the great teacher and the sincere student and give us a clue that we are on the path to the authentic life.

10

THE AUTHENTIC LIFE

The most authentic statement in all of Emerson's works is the following sentence from "Self-Reliance": "Nothing at last is sacred but the integrity of your own mind." He might have said, "Nothing at last is true ... " or "Nothing at last is real ... " but he chose the word "sacred." What is sacred is divine, sanctified, and hallowed. The word usually relates to a place, word, or object. In Exodus 3:5, the voice of God speaks to Moses: "Draw not nigh hither: put off thy shoes from off thy feet; for the place whereon thou standest is holy ground." The sacred is the connection in space and time between heaven and earth, where we encounter the divine. Therefore, in Emerson's statement that crucial connection is placed in the mind. There is no quibbling here, no acquiescence to tradition or fear of heresy.

The key to the statement lies in the relation between what is sacred and what has integrity. In his early (1841) "Lecture on the Times" he said, "I cannot find language of sufficient energy to convey my sense of the sacredness of private integrity." It was the "infinitude of the private man" that he set about to teach, the fact and not the mere speculation of the existence of the soul as an expression of an integrating substance. Since no law can be sacred to Emerson but that of his own mind, it was critical to his vision that he know precisely what integrating the mind involved.

The word "integrity" means wholeness, entireness, completeness, and is related, as well, to purity. A system or entity with integrity is complete, having no part taken away, inoperative or missing. Implied, too, in the word is a perfect state. When Emerson said "Man is a god in ruins," he meant that we had lost our integrity, not so much in the sense of innocence, although that, too, but rather our wholeness. We are fragmented, divided against ourselves and unable to stand erect.

Our aim is to integrate our being "across all these distracting forces" as Emerson said in "Prudence." The ultimate integrity, the true beauty of reality, then, is always unity, within the circle of which man shares his being with divine, eternal, Being. Coming to this singularity of being is the purpose of life, the progress of the soul in matter. Until that integrity is realized, which means made real and made known, the mind continues to live in duality, amid "distracting forces" and without integration.

In a state of duality, even devotion to God (as expressed in the first commandment) lacks integrity—or integration. There is present in that fragmented condition always, as it were, another object of devotion—whatever else is being worshipped in that moment. Objects of worship are many and diverse: sex, entertainment, success, money, recognition, misery, even immortality for the personality. These aspirations—fetishes and graven images—can achieve the status of gods, to be worshipped in their own rituals and ceremonies by millions of people every day. The most common duality in the context of traditional worship is the self-interest of the worshipper, the desire for some benefit to result from the dutiful worship of God as giver of blessings. There is no integrity in such worship, even in the central matter of personal immortality.

When Emerson was asked once about life after death, he said that immortality was for those who were fit for it. His intent in that remark was to suggest that all human beings move in stages and that the soul is "born again," even minute by minute, many times until it finally comes to rest at its source. So, when he said, "A great integrity makes us immortal" ("Immortality"), he expressed something of that stage in the progress of the soul, when it comes, at last, to its natural integrity, or felicity, as Thomas Taylor put it.

What, then, for Emerson is integrity for each individual? The answer to that question is fully and completely expressed in his opening sentence: the integrity of the mind. The integrity implied is not a matter of the narrow self, a reductionist view in which personal conscience, or what seems right to *me*, is the last word, but is rather an affirmation of the capacity of each individual to integrate his or her mind to the Over-Soul, to the final thought, the One Word. All great spiritual teachers insist that true, radical change, or transformation, comes from within. We always begin with the instrument we know the best: our own. For obvious reasons the first step in this process is an awareness that the process wants to take place. In other words, the individual has to make a conscious step in the direction of transformation. This step is most clearly observed in the way we see the activity of our own thoughts. If our thoughts tend to dwell on what we perceive as our own miserable situation, on the offenses that we feel have been heaped upon us from all sides, and if we have the grace and clarity to see that tendency, the opportunity exists to affect a change in that pattern of thought. There is no integrity in moving about the world, accomplishing some task or other, while the mind is preoccupied with fantasies and misery. Even thinking about the meaning and importance of the task we are performing while we are performing it lacks integrity. It is in this sense that we worship a variety of so-called "gods" all the time. In all things, as Shakespeare knew, "thinking makes it so."

THE NATURE OF CONSCIOUSNESS

Philosophical and spiritual traditions provide many definitions of consciousness, of its nature, its presence in human
beings and its ultimate meaning. In many Eastern traditions,
consciousness in its pure form is the same as reality, the material world being an illusion. In the West, consciousness is most
commonly synonymous with awareness of self or ego. Also, it is
sometimes regarded as an organic activity, an energy emanating from the nervous system and brain and having a hierarchy,
as in "sub-," "un-," and "hyper-." As a young man, Emerson
found himself at the close of an age of traditional belief, as the
Enlightenment, with its motto "Dare to know," shattered the
easy reliance on worn and ragged forms. The new emphasis on
the powers of reason as the measure of faith challenged all
thinkers to re-evaluate definitions of the nature of God. As Jeffrey Steele explains,

> As the age became secularized, as belief in divine power
> slowly atrophied, the very analysis of that loss—by positing
> divinity as distant or absent—threatened to promote the
> spiritual decay that it had been designed to retard. By at-
> tempting to name the unnameable, one placed it in a po-
> sition in which it was conditioned by the demands of the
> ego. One read myth literally, instead of as a symbol—such
> was Emerson's recurrent complaint. The trick, instead,
> was to affirm one's connection to hidden centers of spiri-
> tual power without employing terminologies or perspec-
> tives which vitiated them. In response to this crisis,
> Emerson attempted to construct workable attitudes of
> faith in an age when faith itself had started to become
> problematic.[1]

1. Jeffrey Steele, "Interpreting the Self," *Emerson: Prospect and Retrospect,* edited
by Joel Porte (Harvard University Press, 1982) p. 86.

Steele goes on in his valuable essay to make the important connection between "hidden sources of power" and the unconscious realm of the human mind. Unfortunately for the development of this higher dimension, the new mythology which surfaced in the twentieth century to replace traditional beliefs of divine power was seized by Freud and his myths of ego, id, and superego, with all the reductionist implications of his limiting views of the human psyche.

The unconscious, in Freud's hands, became a riot of destructive forces to be managed by the ego and supervised by a fatherly or cultural superego, but all in such banality as to foreclose the possibility of any higher or sublime valuations. Freud's own interpretation of traditional myth exacerbated the problem by placing all unconscious motivation primarily in sexual drives.

More recently, in two books reaching an English-speaking audience only in this decade, have other possibilities begun to emerge. The work of the late Austrian psychoanalyst Paul Diel offers another interpretation of traditional myths in *Symbolism in Greek Mythology: Human Desire and Its Transformations* (Shambhala, 1980). Also, in his *The God-Symbol* (Harper & Row, 1986) Diel redefines aspects of the human psyche to offer an expanded hierarchy which includes a divine element.

> The psyche is not a spacial object divided into compartments. The phrase "psychic process" means nothing more than *particular mode of functioning*. Each process defines a differentiated form of the psychic functioning; it has no existence outside of its way of functioning, and all the psychic processes interact in fluid dynamics. [2]

Given that premise Diel then defines the terms which make up this fluid psyche, as follows:

---

2. Paul Diel, *The God-Symbol* (Harper & Row, 1986), p. 7.

The *conscious* is logical; its tool is language. The unconscious is instinctive and automatic. It already exists at the animal level. The subconscious is an imaginative and symbolizing function. The superconscious is a vague feeling rather than a knowledge. Developed, it is the source of an integrated psychic functioning and the power to harmonize the psychic life. In fact, it is the source of harmony or integration in the mind and has the capability of sublime spiritualization.[3]

Diel's work is important to our consideration of Emerson because we need a broad enough definition of the human psyche with which to translate the language Emerson employed in his definition of consciousness to our own age. Reason, intellect, understanding, intuition, instinct, imagination, and fancy, are all expressions of Emersonian mental life, with Reason being the highest and purest source of revelation. The intellect is Diel's *conscious* dynamic. The intuition is the human faculty which reaches into the realm of Reason, bypassing the intellect, to grasp higher form and content. Emerson's definition of consciousness in "Experience" is very close to Diel's fluid dynamic of the human psyche:

If I have described life as a flux of moods, I must now add that there is in us which changes not and which ranks all sensations and states of mind. The consciousness in each man is a sliding scale, which identifies him now with the First Cause, and now with the flesh of his body; life above life, in infinite degrees.

Emerson says later in the essay that the highest point on the scale is an "unbounded substance."

The form of our thought is the state of consciousness available to us at a given moment. The highest consciousness equals

---

3. Ibid. p.7.

the highest form of being. The universe is a manifestation of consciousness, or can be thought of as a state of consciousness as well. Emersonian thought allows us to integrate the idea of consciousness with the "fact" of a universe. As Emerson suggested in "Worship," a stone in its structure reveals a level of consciousness just as a poem in its structure reveals yet another. The tendency to narrow or expand the degrees of what may or may not be conscious in nature reveals an essential view of the world.

Modern physics has struggled with the relation between energy and matter to the point where most scientists now accept an indefinite border between the two. Passing from one state to another is a continuum of universal expression, and consciousness is both an energy and a substance with the same elasticity of structure. As Joyce demonstrated in *Ulysses*, the conscious life of Leopold Bloom was as valid a form of existence as his wanderings in the streets of Dublin. What Bloom lacked—as do all modern human beings—was the power to integrate consciousness and physical life into an authentic life.

AUTHENTICITY

The authenticity that Emerson struggled to create is bound completely to consciousness as both energy and substance. Authenticity is not measured in events or places or time, but rather depends entirely on the integration of consciousness into the form of the life, which is created daily, moment by moment, and is in its early stages of development easily shattered and fragmented by disturbances. We have to be at once diligent and patient, watchful that the form we are creating is authentic and patient in the face of constant shattering failures.

Evelyn Barish recognizes and celebrates Emerson's contribution to authenticity:

169

He wished to be a prophet, but he was not better than we; he was better than himself, in fact, only in fits and starts, a truth he lamented often enough. But he really was a seer, a see/r in and a see/r out. And he recorded the process of his search in language so intelligent, so delicately tuned to the uncertainties of being in our unanchored and disorderly culture that we go on reading him because his voice is a kind of oboe, an A note against which we tune for authenticity (*Roots of Prophecy*, p. 253).

Many have recognized this tuning to authenticity in Emerson. Few have been so rigorous in their inspirational integrity as he or so consistent over a creative lifetime at the core of that authentic inspiration. Harold Bloom put it simply when he said of Emerson, "He was always right" (*Emerson*, p.2).

But as Barish also points out, Emerson was a see/r rather than a hear/er, thus making his A note a matter of sighted authenticity. As he said of himself in a notebook entry,

> I think sometimes that my lack of a musical ear is made good to me through my eyes. That which others hear, I *see*. All the soothing, plaintive, brisk or romantic moods, which corresponding melodies waken in them, I find in the carpet of the wood, in the margin of the pond, in the shade of the hemlock grove, or in the infinite variety & rapid dance of the treetops, as I hurry along.

There is a danger in this romanticizing, however, as Emerson well understood. The test of authenticity had to be rigorous indeed when the eyes or the ears were captured by shifting moods. At the same time that Emerson could glory in nature on a walk toward Fairhaven with Henry Thoreau, admiring the "autumnal red & yellow" he could warn himself that "A walk in the woods is only an exalted dream" (*Emerson in His Journals*, p. 226).

There are illusions of authenticity, as Emerson was quick to note. In moments of peace and tranquility, in a beautiful natural setting, the mind may be able to expand to the visible horizon and beyond, be conscious of drifts of air and the stirrings of leaves. In those moments, the narrow sense of self may subside for a moment, broadening to something more universal, creating a new sensation, but we should not be deceived. It is what Emerson meant by the exalted dream.

This narrow perception is a form of spiritual longing, nothing more or less. It has no more reality than any other illusion, but it has subtle qualities that make us think it is authentic. Our true business lies in watching this form of movement in the mind and in answering nature when it calls us to attention. When Emerson described the cry of the eagle awakening him to thought as he dreamed through the woods, he was making a critical distinction between an illusory and an authentic state of consciousness.

THE WISH TO SERVE

Although Emerson described the Transcendentalist as one who waits upon the world to call him or her to attention, he also was clear about what constituted the responsible life in the culture. We are servants of a will greater than our own, seeking to know and to respond to that will. The wish to serve, "to add somewhat to the well-being of men" was Emerson's way of drawing the attention away from selfish concerns in order that we might experience a shift in the state of being. Service provides the means of integrating the inner and outer worlds by involving the mind in the world and diverting it from the personal gods of immediate desire.

Those who become conscious of another level of being, namely, an intense inner life, may begin to see the ordinary world of work as an encumbrance, wondering what work has to do with inner development, with the spiritual life? The following description of this conflict comes from the essay "Success," which Emerson delivered in December, 1858 in

Hartford, Connecticut. (The essay is not contained in most anthologies, appearing only in Volume VII of the *Works of Emerson.*)

We live on different planes or platforms. There is an external life, which is educated at school, taught to read, write, cipher and trade; taught to grasp all the boy can get, urging him to put himself forward, to make himself useful and agreeable in the world, to ride, run, argue and contend, unfold his talents, shine, conquer and possess.

But the inner life sits at home, and does not learn to do things, nor value these feats at all. 'Tis a quiet, wise perception. It loves truth, because it is itself real; it loves right, it knows nothing else; but it makes no progress; was as wise in our first memory of it as now; is just the same now in maturity and hereafter in age, as it was in youth. We have grown to manhood and womanhood; we have powers, connection, children, reputations, professions: this makes no account of them all. It lives in the great present; it makes the present great. This tranquil, well-founded, wide-seeing soul is no express-rider, no attorney, no magistrate: it lies in the sun and broods on the world.

This brooding on the world carries with it a sense of the dualism of the inner and outer worlds. When we acquire some sense of this wide-seeing soul, we mimic it with our own brooding, as in the sense of self-consciousness. We become philosophers, detached, self-aware, thinkers on the ineffable, knowers of the unknowable; in other words, full of conflict. Emerson explored this conflict in great detail in "The Transcendentalist" (1841), written to explain to a wider audience the life and thought of his Concord circle. At the heart of his description is a paragraph which describes the conflict inherent in this inner life:

It is not to be denied that there must be some wide difference between my faith and other faith; and mine is a certain brief experience, which surprised me in the highway or in the market, in some place, at some time,—whether in the body or out of the body, God knoweth,—and made me aware that I had played the fool with fools all this time, but that law existed for me and for all; that to me belongeth trust, a child's trust and obedience, and the worship of ideas, and I should never be fool more. Well, in the space of an hour probably, I was let down from this height; I was at my old tricks, the selfish member of a selfish society.

The mention of surprise is a reminder of the role which grace plays in the first moments of faith. What follows involves realization, obedience, and trust, but the beginning is grace, and always has been. Emerson goes on to develop his description of duality:

The worst feature of this double consciousness is, that the two lives, of the understanding and of the soul, which we lead, really show very little relation to each other; one prevails now, all buzz and din; and the other prevails then, all infinitude and paradise; and, with the progress of life, the two discover no greater disposition to reconcile themselves.

Reconciliation is, however, possible. If the search is genuine, the conflict is reduced. The resolution lies in work, the daily activity we find to do in the world. Work is both the task we perform for remuneration and the life we lead each day. In spiritual circles the word "work" is often used to denote the conscious application of practices to the development of God-knowing. That kind of "practice" can be combined with so-called ordinary work by the way in which the mind perceives the nature of the tasks being performed in our vocations.

173

Ordinary work and spiritual practice find their point of convergence, their identity, in the idea and fact of work as service. The line of convergence to that point is the discovery of the work we are meant to do. When we are engaged in our proper work, the faith and trust we found in revelation, momentary though it might have been, is experienced again as a timeless concentration in the mind upon the task at hand. We are a part and particle of God-in-the-life. Those who know this fact speak of the wonder they experience in times of focused attention, when clarity of thought opens a flow of energy like a channel to the sea.

That image appears in "Spiritual Laws" as part of the discussion about talent and the discovery of our work in the world:

> This talent and this call depend on his organization, or the mode in which the general soul incarnates itself in him. He inclines to do something which is easy to him and good when it is done, but which no other man can do. He has no rival. For the more truly he consults his own powers, the more difference will his work exhibit from the work of any other. His ambition is exactly proportioned to his powers. The height of the pinnacle is determined by the breadth of the base. . . . By doing his work he makes the need felt which he can supply, and creates the taste by which he is enjoyed. By doing his own work he unfolds himself.

The "organization" spoken of in the passage must be the subject of self-examination. Before we exercise our talents, express our ambition, set our sights, there must be the knowledge of how the "general soul incarnates itself" in us. Much of that consideration depends upon both the constitution (how we are constituted by nature) and temperament (how we respond to the demands of nature). Emerson suggests that the expression of our native talent is fundamentally easy, in the sense of natural; it is a gift. We may be able to move with grace, power or with minute control. We may have a gift for stillness, for fine perception or for sensitivity. Music may flow from our fingers or our mind. Animals may become still and obedient in our presence, or the intricacies of machinery may reveal themselves to us. We may have the gift of eloquence, or of prophecy, or of leadership. We may have a talent for details or for principles. Talent is the diversity that nature and civilization have made manifest.

Once the talent is recognized and developed through discipline and practice, we find that we want to find an original application. We do not want simply to repeat what others have done. "For the more truly he consults his own powers, the more difference will his work exhibit from the work of any other" ("Spiritual Laws"). The aim is to discover and then cultivate an authentic freedom.

FREEDOM AND AUTHENTICITY

There are as many pitfalls in the pursuit of freedom as there are in the pursuit of authenticity. First, there is the relationship between freedom and originality. Lack of originality may indicate a fear of freedom. Even when we have found our teachers, we need, eventually, to deny our precursors in favor of a purer source of inspiration. Walt Whitman denied Emerson as an influence when he knew that his own expression would be diminished if Emerson was identified with him too closely as a source of inspiration. Emerson himself referred to his own precursors as "lustres," shining moments in his experience to light his own journey, but he also understood the dangers of dependence. He wrote in his journal: "It is the necessity of my nature to shed all influences" (*JMN*, VII, 326). Integrity demands such distancing from our sources.

A danger in the search for freedom, however, is denying one's teachers too soon. To do so may preclude the development of a greater freedom later on. There are too many artists,

175

for example, who flee their teachers in favor of a limited freedom, with the result that their work exhibits nothing but the agony of that premature flight. Too many students act upon feelings of rebellion before they have acquired any integrity as thinkers, with the result that their expression is confined to the only theme they know, which is their rebellion. There is no integrity in rebellion per se.

Authenticity in the realm of spirit has the same aim, namely the discovery of a genuine freedom in our relation to divinity. In "The Over-Soul" Emerson said, "When we have broken our god of tradition and ceased from our god of rhetoric, then may God fire the heart in his presence," thereby giving a personal relevance to Jesus's declaration that "The father and I are one." What we seek in this struggle is an identity. No longer in matters of identity is this thing like that thing, nor is a human being in the image of God; rather, at the vanishing point of resemblance we arrive at an integrity which is perfect, being whole.

A paradox remains at the center of the search for an authentic life. We have to break, lovingly, the vessels of our tradition in order to become one with the source of that tradition. In that space there is no center toward which we can consciously strive, nor is there an outer boundary to force or breach. There is only the sea of consciousness where we exist, doing the work we have been given to do. When our vessel finds the channel down the river of life to that sea, it is broken where the fresh water and salt water mix, and the contents are loosed to their element, water to water, soul to soul. It is an image of both dissolution and of unity, the paradox of identity.

When we find ourselves confronting this paradox, seeking reconciliation in conscious hours, we are able to draw for support upon the power of Emerson's vision. Our moments of connection to the sublime may be momentary, caught by surprise, clouded by considerations, and diminished by doubts, but they are real nonetheless, and they are the source of our self-recovery.

In dedication to Emerson, we give him the last word, from "Worship":

And so I think that the last lesson of life, the choral song which rises from all elements and all angels, is a voluntary obedience, a necessitated freedom. Man is made of the same atoms as the world is, he shares the same impressions, predispositions, and destiny. When his mind is illuminated, when his heart is kind, he throws himself joyfully into the sublime order, and does, with knowledge, what the stones do by structure.

Selected Glossary

This brief glossary of terms used by Emerson in his work
may serve to clarify his thought.

Art : *the soul's action on the world; to educate the perception of beauty.*

Beauty : *the underlying likenesses of the beautiful.*

Behavior : *my manner of life.*

Body : *my office, where I work.*

Character : *a reserved force which acts directly by presence;
a latent power.*

Considerations : *the positive centers of my actions.*

Civilization : *the powers of a good woman.*

Culture : *my widest sympathies and affinities.*

Dialectic : *to Platonize: to drive through a subject to its essence.*

Ethics : *the soul illustrated in daily life.*

Existence : *the soul's need for an organ in nature.*

Fate : *the limitations of my inheritance and the natural world.*

Freedom : *without any hindrance that does not arise out of my own
constitution.*

Generalization : *a new influx of divinity into the mind.*

History : *the record of the works of the universal mind.*

Illusions : *the games and masks of my self-deception.*

179

Instinct : *revelations of the soul in the mind.*

Intellect : *the organ which sees an object as it stands in the light of science. Cool and disengaged.*

Intuition : *An insight into the perfection of the laws of the soul.*

Jesus : *(his purpose) to redeem us from a formal religion; to teach us to seek our well-being in the formation of the soul; the mediator who instructs man to become like God.*

Literature : *the soul's record in the world; a platform whence we may command a view of our present life; a purchase by which we may move it.*

Logic : *the procession or proportionate unfolding of the intuition.*

Love of Truth : *abstaining from dogmatism, recognizing the opposite negations between which the being is swung; respect for the highest law of being.*

Man (human being) : *a stupendous antagonism, a dragging together of the poles of the universe; a god in ruins.*

Manners : *silent and mediate expressions of the soul.*

Nature : *an endless combination and repetition of a very few laws.*

Obedience : *the eye which reads the laws of the universe.*

Philosophy : *the account which the human mind gives to itself of the constitution of the world.*

Politics : *the activity of the soul illustrated in power.*

Power : *my abilities and energies.*

Purpose of the World : *to realize the transformation of genius into practical power.*

Religion : *the emotion of reverence inspired by the soul.*

Repose : *God offers to every mind its choice between truth and repose. Synonymous with ignorance.*

Science : *the discovery of the soul's methods.*

Soul : *not an organ but animates the organs; not a function but uses function; not a faculty but a light; not intellect or will but the master of the intellect and the will; it is related to the world.*

180

Teaching : *he who gives, and he learns who receives; there is no teaching until the pupil is brought into the same state or principle in which you are; a transfusion takes place; he is you and you are he; then is a teaching.*

Thinking : *a pious reception.*

Trades : *the learning of the soul in nature by labor.*

Transcendentalism : *Intuitive thought. Also, Idealism.*

Virtue : *the adherence in action to the nature of things; a perpetual substitution of being for seeming.*

Wealth : *my gains and losses.*

Wisdom : *To finish the moment, to find the journey's end in every step of the road; to live the greatest number of good hours.*

Worship : *my belief.*

Works Cited

Allen, Gay, *Waldo Emerson*, New York, 1981.

Barish, Evelyn, *Emerson: The Roots of Prophecy*, Princeton, 1989.

Bishop, Johnathan, *Emerson on the Soul*, Cambridge, 1964.

Bloom, Harold, *Agon*, Oxford, 1982.
—*The Breaking of the Vessels*, Chicago, 1982.
—*Ralph Waldo Emerson*, New York, 1985.

Bode, Carl, ed., *Ralph Waldo Emerson: A Profile*, New York, 1968.

Cabot, James Elliot, *A Memoir of Ralph Waldo Emerson*, 2 vol.,
London, 1887.

Cudworth, Ralph, *The True Intellectual System of the Universe*,
London, 1678.

Emerson, Ralph Waldo, *Works of Emerson*, 12 vols., Boston, 1903.
—*The Journals and Miscellaneous Notebooks of Ralph Waldo Emerson*,
ed. William Gilman, et al., 16 vols., Cambridge, 1960-1982.
—*The Letters of Ralph Waldo Emerson*, ed. Ralph L. Rusk, 6 vols.,
New York, 1939.

Holmes, Oliver Wendell *Ralph Waldo Emerson*, Boston, 1885.

Konvitz, Milton, ed., *The Recognition of Ralph Waldo Emerson*,
Ann Arbor, 1972.

Levin, David, ed., *Emerson: Prophecy, Metamorphosis, and Influence*, New
York, 1975.

Nozick, Robert, *The Examined Life*, New York, 1989.

Pagels, Elaine, *The Gnostic Gospels*, New York, 1979.

Pieper, Josef, *Leisure: The Basis of Culture*, New York, 1963.

Porte, Joel, *Emerson: Prospect and Retrospect*, Cambridge, 1982.

—*Emerson in His Journals*, Cambridge, 1982.

Smith, John, *Select Discourses*, London, 1660.

Taylor, Thomas, *Works of Plato*, 5 vols., London, 1804.

Thoreau, Henry, *Walden*, New York, 1963.

Index

About the Author

RICHARD GELDARD is the author of *The Traveller's Key to Greece*. He teaches at Yeshiva College in New York and lectures on Emerson and sacred studies at such places as the New York Open Center. He received his master's degree in English from the Bread Loaf School of Middlebury College and his doctorate in literature and classics from Stanford University.